THE VIRGIN INTERNET SHOPPING GUIDE

THE VIRGIN INTERNET SHOPPING GUIDE

VERSION 2.0

Simon Collin

Virgin

First published in Great Britain in 1999 by
Virgin Publishing Ltd
Thames Wharf Studios
Rainville Road
London W6 9HA

Version 2.0 – November 2000

Printed and bound by Omnia Books Ltd, Glasgow

ISBN 0 7535 0540 1

A catalogue record for this book is available from the British Library.

//LET US HELP YOU TO FIND THE BEST ON THE NET

'Buy it online from our website'

'It's much cheaper on the web'

'Visit shops around the world'

The Internet is probably the most important consumer revolution of our lifetimes. Yet it's managed to sneak up behind most of us – and many of our leading retailers – and take us by surprise. We're now waking up to the simple fact that for many goods, the Internet is a better way to buy and sell.

In some areas, online shops have grown so fast, they've outpaced traditional market leaders. Bookselling, for example, was turned on its head by the arrival of Amazon.com, which within a few years was worth more than Barnes and Noble – a traditional, long-established chain with over 300 stores.

Electronic commerce had a difficult birth, largely because nobody trusted the net with bank or credit card details. Now there's a range of reliable high-security systems that make buying on the net safer than over the phone or in a local shop. And it's usually cheaper. An Internet shop doesn't have to rent a high street property and it doesn't need any shop assistants, so its overheads are tiny. And many firms are offering deep discounts simply in order to get your custom.

We'll show you where to go and how to buy, talk you through the online auction experience and teach you how to use special tools to scour the shops for the lowest prices. We include everything you need to know about security, consumer rights and even import duty for overseas purchases.

This book starts with some simple advice about buying equipment and getting online, but it isn't just for beginners. It's also for the millions of people who are overwhelmed or frustrated by the sheer size and complexity of what's out there. At its heart is a list of the most useful, secure online shops around the world that ship to the UK – all wonderful springboards from which to dive in and start shopping.

Let The Virgin Internet Shopping Guide show you around the biggest mall in the world.

Simon Collin, who compiled this guide, is a technology writer and net-obsessive who has worked for many of the leading computer magazines and has written over two dozen books about computing and the Internet.

The Internet is evolving so fast that, even though this book was correct at the time of going to press, there could be a few dud addresses or omissions. If you have any problems with anything in this book, send us an email at **response@virgin-pub.co.uk**. We'll make sure it's dealt with in the next edition.

//CONTENTS

1//GETTING ONLINE

Before you can start to explore the Internet, you've got to get online. This can be the most difficult part of the whole process – and it normally causes people the most headaches. Once you have chosen a computer, you will also need to set up an account with a company called an Internet service provider (ISP) that supplies you with a route on to the net. Finally, you will need to install and configure special software to work with this company (although almost all new computers now come with all the software pre-installed, so there you'll face just a few steps before getting online).

This chapter tells you what equipment you'll need, how to choose it and how to set it all up.

//WHAT SORT OF COMPUTER DO I NEED?

In theory, any computer can be connected to the Internet – from a high-powered graphics workstation to a pocket-sized personal organiser. Using the Internet is not particularly demanding on your computer's resources. Most computers can be coaxed into going online, but if you've a computer that's over three years old, you'll find that your Internet provider is unlikely to support the special software you need. If you bought your computer new within the last year, you'll have no problems getting online. If you're still shopping for a new system, here are the basic guidelines you should follow.

When you buy a new computer, you have two basic choices: do you buy a PC-compatible or a Macintosh? The two options provide different ways of designing what's inside the computer, what sort of central processor chip is used and what sort of software can be run. In practice, PCs dominate through sheer range of software and accessories. Macintosh computers tend to look nicer but any extra software or hardware can be more expensive. Software and hardware for one type doesn't easily work on the other platform.

You don't need to invest before you surf. For just a few pounds, your local library provides very cheap access to the net, or if you want help and a coffee, try a local Internet café.

PC-compatibles Ensure that you're getting Windows 98 or 2000 pre-installed. You need a reasonably fast processor: anything running at 250MHz or faster will be adequate. You'll need at least 32Mb of main memory (RAM) – most new PCs are supplied with 64Mb. Buy the biggest hard disk you can afford: however big the disk, it'll soon fill up so ensure you've got at least 4–6Gb on board. Lastly, get a monitor and graphics adapter that can display images at a resolution of at least 800x600 (most web pages are designed to be displayed at this resolution).

Macintosh Make sure you have System 8 installed (you can make do with 7.5 but anything older is hard work). Any new Mac will be running a PowerPC processor. For those who prefer the Macintosh experience, the price of new Macs – notably the Internet-ready (and cute with it) iMac – has dropped dramatically. Aim for at least 32Mb of main memory, though 64Mb is preferred. Your hard disk should have a capacity of at least 4–6Gb and the graphics adapter/monitor combination needs to support a minimum resolution of 800x600 with 256 or more colours.

Mobile phones The newest breed of UK and European mobile phones use WAP (wireless application protocol) – a system that lets you send and read email messages and browse websites. WAP-compatible phones tend to be a little bigger than standard mobile phones, to accommodate the larger display screen and navigation keys. However, the display can still only show a few lines of text or very basic black-and-white images.

Each WAP phone and network has a different way of configuring and connecting your phone to the net – you'll need to read the instructions carefully or, better still, ask your phone dealer to set it up for you.

Once you are online, you are limited to the painfully slow connection speed of 9.6Kbps. But still, it's fine for reading short email messages and checking weather, share prices or news headlines. You can't always access standard websites – instead you'll have to start searching for special WAP-sites that have been created using the WML (WAP markup language) system. Visit portals such as WAP.com (**www.wap.com**) and WAP Forum (**www.wapforum.com**) for a directory of what's available online.

//HOW DO I CONNECT?

Before you set out to explore, you need to link your computer to the net. Your shopping list has three items on it:

- a box that connects your computer to the phone line (called the modem)
- a normal telephone line (you can always upgrade later)
- an account with a company called an Internet service provider (ISP), which provides a doorway to the Internet for the general public

Modems

You need a modem (short for modulator-demodulator) in order to convert the digital data from your computer into analogue sound that can then be sent over a standard phone line. They also need sophisticated features to cut out the hiss, crackle and pops you normally hear on a line that would otherwise scramble data.

New PCs are now almost always sold with a modem fitted. You can get modems tucked away inside your computer (an internal model) or in the form of a little box that connects to the serial port at the back of your computer (an external model). Both models do the same job – an external model is a little more expensive but it's easier to move from one machine to another if you upgrade. If your new computer doesn't include an internal modem as part of the bundle, a fast high-spec modem will cost between £50–100. Spend your money on speed rather than dinky features like an answering machine or sculpted casing.

Modems are cheap, work with your existing phone line and let you connect to any Internet service provider. On the downside, they are relatively slow and can take up to a minute to go through the tedious business of actually dialling and connecting to the Internet.

Modem standards, which define the speed at which a modem can transfer information, are always on the move, constantly being developed and improved. Within a year, your new modem will be considered as slow as a ... well ... a very slow thing. To get out of this trap, check that the modem supports software upgrades (often called Flash-ROM or Flash upgrades). Whenever a new specification is developed, log on to the modem manufacturer's website and follow the instructions: new configuration data will be automatically transferred to the modem and it'll run at the new speed. That's the theory and, at least with the big modem makers such as Hayes, 3Com and US Robotics, it's true.

If you're feeling ambitious, you can tie together two modems (with a second special box of electronics) to effectively double your speed. Windows users already have the software to support this Multilink standard, but you'll need to talk nicely to your Internet provider before you do this as very few ISPs support the standard.

And, in practice, no one actually ever does this because it's cheaper to upgrade to the faster ISDN communications system.

When buying a modem, refer to the following checklist:

1 Buy the fastest modem you can. Make sure it supports a transfer rate of 56Kbps (the current standard is called V90).

2 Ensure it supports upgrades to Flash-ROM so you can keep up with the latest standard.

3 Some modems include a built-in answering machine – do you really want to pay extra for this? Unlikely.

4 Almost all modems are capable of sending and receiving faxes – it's a nice extra that shouldn't cost any more.

5 Internal modems are cheaper but are more difficult to install.

6 In the UK, make sure it's BABT-approved (the box will display a sticker with a round green spot) that legally lets you connect it to your telephone socket.

How fast is fast?

The speed of a communications channel describes the amount of information that it can carry every second – the maximum is called its 'bandwidth'. The speed is usually described with the 'Kbps' or 'Mbps' acronym. Kbps (Kilobits Per Second) describes the number of thousand individual pieces of digital information that can be transferred every second. Mbps (Megabits Per Second) is faster and describes the number of million individual pieces of digital information transferred per second.

A fast modem, for example, will be described as 56Kbps. It can, in theory, send 56,000 individual pieces of digital information every second (each is called a 'bit' of data); sometimes, this number is rewritten and described as 'bandwidth' – in this case, it means the same thing.

The theoretical maximum speed of your modem is just one factor in deciding the real speed of the connection. You need a good, clear telephone line and an ISP that uses the same high-speed modems. In practice, you'll never hit the maximum speed of your modem; instead, you'll generally cruise at somewhere between 60–80% of the maximum.

Faster, faster

Most people connect to the net using a modem, but it's hardly the fastest technology available. You could upgrade to Home Highway, but if you plan to use the Internet every day or you have your own busy website to manage, you might consider upgrading to a faster connection.

Each of the following technologies will cost you more than a standard modem connection. First, you'll need a new box to link your computer to the new communications channel and, second, the monthly rental is generally higher than a standard phone line. Lastly, every ISP supports links via a modem, but not all support these higher-speed technologies.

Fed up with slow response? Internet 2 is being developed and this will zing along at a fantastic rate. For more information, visit the website: www.internet2.org

ISDN (Integrated Services Digital Network) is an all-digital high-speed alternative to a modem; it easily outpaces even the fastest modem and can make the call and connect you to the Internet in less than a second. In the UK there's a big push from telcos (telephone companies) to increase the number of customers (primarily businesses) that connect via ISDN. In the US and elsewhere in the world, it's still an eccentric technology that is about to be outpaced by the cable technology described below.

Most UK residents can get an ISDN line delivered to their home or office. The installation charge is normally high but the phone calls should cost the same as with a standard telephone line. All the main telephone companies and cable TV companies can install an ISDN line, but they'll charge you different rates. Once you've got an ISDN line, you can link your computer to the line with the ISDN equivalent of a modem – called a terminal adapter (TA).

Once you have an ISDN line, you need to ask your ISP for a special ISDN dial-up account. Most providers, including the free ISPs, do support ISDN. Currently, AOL and CompuServe don't.

Home Highway

Home Highway is a cut-down British version of ISDN that's easier to understand and cheaper to install than the digital system and is still faster than a modem.

The problem for BT is that once it announces full access to ADSL (see page 8), it will probably be forced to stop supplying the slower Home Highway system.

To get started, call BT to ask if Home Highway is available in your area. If it is, your old line will be converted to two digital lines (with two numbers) and you'll get a neat box in the corner of your room. Plug in your old phone and your new ISDN terminal adapter (TA) to connect your computer and you're off. Dedicated surfers will like Home Highway but there's better technology around the corner.

Cable modem If you have cable TV running into your home, you're looking at the best route to potential high-speed Internet access with little effort and cost. We say 'potential' because it depends entirely on the whim of your cable provider.

A cable modem sits between your computer and the raw cable from the cable TV company. You'll need the cable modem itself (called a head-end) and a network adapter card for your computer. Once you're set up, you have the potential to use the full capacity of the cable (or, at any rate, what's left after sending down the TV channel you're watching). You'll also have to share this capacity with other users in your area but it's still a mighty fast link from home to net. In practice, you could expect to receive data at up to 10Mbps (almost 200 times faster than a standard modem) – though a more realistic figure is likely to be around 2Mbps (still a respectable 40 times faster). When sending information to the Internet, you use a slower channel over the same cable, running at a maximum of around 128Kbps.

The biggest providers in the UK, Cable & Wireless (**www.cwcom.co.uk**), NTL (**www.ntl.co.uk**) and Telewest (**www.telewest.co.uk**), have begun to carry out trials in some areas, but you'll have to call to ask when this might happen near you. Keep in touch with developments via the Cable Communications Association (**www.cable.co.uk**) and read about the first cable modems from 3Com (**www.3com.com**) and Motorola (**www.mot.com**).

DSL and ADSL ISDN's new cousin, DSL (Digital Subscriber Lines), is beginning to appear. It's another way of providing a high-speed digital link to the Internet but its great advantage is that it can work over standard telephone cabling. There are several different versions of DSL technology with ADSL (Asymmetric Digital

Subscriber Lines) just around the corner and even a reality in many countries.

Like ISDN, you'll need a special adapter that connects your computer to the line. Unlike ISDN, ADSL uses your original telephone cable but can pump data along the wire at an astonishingly fast rate. It can send data from the Internet to your computer at a staggering 32Mbps (that's 50 times faster than basic ISDN) and lets you transmit data on to the Internet at a variable rate of between 32Kbps and 1Mbps. This split rate works fine in practice as you'll normally receive far more information than you send.

The second main difference is that ADSL is 'always on'; this means that you effectively have a permanent connection to the Internet – for home users, this means no delays when dialling, and for business users it means the chance to set up their own server. Instead of paying for calls by the minute, you pay a flat, fixed monthly rental. In some countries this is affordable for home enthusiasts, but in the UK the price is between £40–150 per month – more than you could ever run up on the phone bill.

There are few problems with ADSL. The main catch is availability. You need to have a local phone company that supports the system and you need to be near the exchange – it supports a maximum distance of around three miles from exchange to home. Lastly, you also need an ISP that supports ADSL (the main business ISPs and many of the larger home-user ISPs all support ADSL).

In the United States, most areas have only patchy coverage. In the UK, it's been trialled and is now available in most parts of the country – but you'll need to check with BT or Cable & Wireless if your area is connected.

If you do get set up with ADSL, it should cost no more to install than an existing ISDN line. The terminal adapter will be a little more expensive (around £150) and running costs are built into the monthly rental charge.

Leased line If you're running a large company – or your own popular website – you might consider a permanent line from your office to the ISP. This is called a leased line – it's your own dedicated, direct link. You don't dial a number as you're always online. This is not really an option for any home user and your telco would probably laugh if you asked.

Once the pavement's been dug-up and the cable installed, you can subscribe to different levels of service. Each level (normally designated by 'T' numbers in the US and 'transfer rates' in the UK) provides different transmission speeds for data and is charged at basic rental plus monthly subscription. You'll also need a special account from your ISP. Most users can't even consider leased lines – but at least you know they exist!

Satellite Yes, you can use a direct satellite link to connect to the Internet. The main service provider is DirecPC (**www.direcpc.com**) who install a dish on your roof and direct it to the right spot in the sky. Oddly, the service can only send you information; you can't transmit back (you'd need something similar to Goonhilly for satellite transmissions). Instead, your computer is linked up to a standard modem that's used with your normal phone line. The description makes it all sound rather clunky but it works fine in practice and provides an alternative, high-speed route to the Internet.

Why is it so slow?

To get the best performance from your Internet connection, it's worth knowing what can cause the traffic jams and so the sluggish performance you'll experience when using the net. Your computer's speed and power is not really relevant, but the connection to the net is very important.

The speed of your modem determines how fast you can transfer information to and from your computer. But even with a high-speed modem you could still suffer. You are at the mercy of congestion on the backbone (the motorway that links your Internet provider to all the other providers). As more users log in at peak time, the motorway chokes up – so avoid early evening or your local time equivalent to when the United States wakes up.

Even with a clear run on the main route across the Internet, you still need the equivalent of fast local roads. Your link to your ISP needs to be fast and so does the ISP's link to the backbone. And lastly, if you're trying to view a website, you have to be sure that their computer is fast, their link to their ISP is fast and that their ISP has a good connection to the main backbone.

//CHOOSING AN INTERNET SERVICE PROVIDER

Your computer's running. The modem's plugged in. Now you need to choose an Internet Service Provider (ISP). An ISP works as a necessary middleman; it provides a local telephone number for your modem to dial to connect to their big computers that form part of the Internet. Only the very biggest sites or corporations link directly to the Internet while everyone else makes use of ISPs and leaves them to manage the techie network connections.

Choosing an ISP can be a problem. Some are vast international companies that are financially and technically solid, provide great support and a good service. Others are two-bit fly-by-nights who could go bust or could ruin your surfing experience by providing crummy service. To help you choose the right provider, run through the questions given on page 15.

Check that your intended Internet provider supports local-rate calls in your area or you'll end up with a vast phone bill each month.

What's the difference between the ISPs?

There are lots of different ways of grouping and classifying ISPs but, essentially, there are now just two types of company: one charges and the other is free. Why, you're wondering, can some companies still get away with charging for Internet access when there are so many free services? Your first instinct might be to plump for the free service, but you might find that you're better served by one of the companies that charge. Here are the main differences.

Free ISPs

Some countries, notably the UK, have such aggressive marketing from telephone companies and ISPs that you can now sign up for free Internet access. A free ISP generally specialises in home and personal users and provides local-rate access numbers in a particular region. You don't pay any monthly subscription, just the usual telephone charges. In return, you get web space, an email account, access to newsgroups and free software to get you started.

These companies survive by selling advertising or by splitting the profit on the cost of the phone call with the telephone company. Slim margins, but still profitable.

A couple of ISPs are even experimenting with providing free Internet access and free phone calls. Scour the newspapers for details – they are normally heavily promoted to boost the profile of the ISP and only available at certain times of the week (such as the weekend).

Pros: it's free!

Cons: can be very busy in the evenings and weekends, making it hard to get online. You might have to put up with extra advertisements and you cannot run a business or create cutting-edge websites – though you can create simple websites for free.

Why pay?

The majority of ISPs still charge a monthly subscription fee to connect you to the Internet. For your money (normally between £5–10 per month) you get full access to the Internet (just like a free ISP) but there are several extra benefits: first, there's no advertising – just the plain Internet. Second, you should be able to create a more sophisticated website of your own and, third, you should also receive a handful of email addresses for you and your family.

Plus, if you're just starting out, you might need to call technical support if your computer refuses to connect. Free ISPs often charge premium rates to reach technical support – you should receive free 24-hour support from an ISP that is charging you a monthly subscription.

Many ISPs are now re-aligning themselves to provide e-commerce and other business-related extras – to allow companies to register their own, unique identity on the Internet (called their domain name) or set up a shopping site.

Pros: free support, rarely hit an engaged tone and the only route to setting up a sophisticated or business website.

Cons: costs a monthly subscription fee.

Content providers

Some ISPs provide much more than a 'plain vanilla' connection to the Internet. In addition to the full access to the net, you can also use the company's own, internal database – a sort of private Internet for subscribers. There are plenty of ISPs that have set up to publish their own content; AOL, CompuServe, LineOne and Virgin Net. To confuse matters, some content providers charge a subscription, while others are free (see the list at the end of this chapter for full details).

AOL and CompuServe

The two biggest ISPs in the world are AOL and CompuServe (AOL owns CompuServe) – AOL alone has 16 million subscribers. These two companies take a different route to providing Internet access to subscribers. They are both content providers – they have put a huge amount of effort into building up their own private community for subscribers that's like a mini-Internet: it's got news, sport, music, reviews, games, and lots of discussion groups and chat rooms.

In addition to this extra content, you can also use the company's international network of telephone access numbers – which is great for travellers but not relevant to anyone else. For example, if you want to check your email when you're on holiday in Spain, you use the local access number for Spain – with a standard ISP you would need to make a long-distance call back to your normal access number.

Take advantage of AOL and CompuServe by picking up one of the free CDs that are in just about every computer magazine and giving each a trial run – both offer a free one-month trial period. If you don't like it, don't continue your subscription.

The other main difference is that you use custom-written software that attempts to make your Internet experience as foolproof as possible. This custom software includes useful features for families: parents can define the type of content their children can view.

AOL has two different ways of charging for its services. Either pay a low monthly subscription, which includes a quota of a few hours online (you'll pay by the minute once you've used up this quota), or pay a higher subscription for unlimited time online. To add a degree of confusion, AOL has launched its own free ISP service, called Netscape Online (**www.netscapeonline.co.uk**), but this is not the same as the original AOL and doesn't have the custom software, discussion groups or parental control.

Choosing an ISP

We've listed the major national ISPs in the Address Book at the end of this chapter. You'll find hundreds of local ISPs near you that offer great service but might not have the technical infrastructure to give you the fastest connection to the Internet. Free ISPs are great for home use but have a limited range of advanced features.

Who's going to get your account? Is it to be a free ISP or a global giant like AOL? To help you decide, have a look at the statements below, and see which one(s) apply to you:

1. 'I'm stingy' – go for an ISP that offers free Internet access (see the Address Book at the end of this chapter).
2. 'I'm stingy and broke' – go for an ISP that offers free Internet access and free phone calls.
3. 'I've a reputation to maintain' – go for an established national or international ISP.
4. 'I want to set up a website for my business' – you'll get better service from a standard ISP that charges.
5. 'I only plan to surf during evenings and weekends' – you'll have a few busy signals from free ISPs during peak time.
6. 'I want my own domain name, ISDN and lots of support' – a standard charging ISP is best for all this.

7 'I don't want busy signals' – make sure the ISP has no more than 10 users per modem (ask them for this ratio).

8 'I want to connect with Home Highway or ISDN' – most ISPs, including the free ones, support this but ask first to make sure.

9 'I want to create my own online shop' – your only option is an ISP that charges.

10 'I want to check my email as I travel around the world' – your best bet is an account with AOL or CompuServe that you can access anywhere, or to sign up for a free web-based email service (see page xxx).

11 'I want to surf each night till my eyelids droop' – avoid CompuServe and other ISPs that charge by the minute. Choose either a free or charging ISP that doesn't limit your time online.

12 'I don't want to worry about configuring things, so just get me online quickly' – almost all major ISPs have easy-to-install software that loads automatically from a CD-ROM.

//SETTING UP YOUR COMPUTER

To use the Internet you need to install and configure special software on your computer. Setting everything up is normally very easy and takes just a few minutes. Best of all, most friendly ISPs will send you a starter-pack and CD-ROM when you subscribe – this includes pre-configured versions of all the essential software that you will need. If you don't have a CD-ROM, you can still get online as almost all the software you need is pre-loaded in every new PC (it's part of Windows or the Macintosh operating system bundle) – but you will need to configure it correctly.

If you have decided to use AOL, CompuServe or an ISP that supplies a complete installation kit, simply insert the CD-ROM they sent you and follow the simple instructions – the software configures your computer and takes you online.

If you're setting up an older computer (pre-Windows 95 or Macintosh System 8), you'll need special software that isn't normally provided by the ISP. Ask them for the correct version when you subscribe – they should have software available to get you online. Otherwise, buy an Internet-related magazine that has a free CD stuck to the front-cover – these CDs usually have a library of software that's enough to get you started.

Get ready to connect

When you subscribe to an ISP, you'll be sent a list of configuration details that need to be typed in to set up your computer so it knows how to connect to the net. (If you've subscribed to AOL, CompuServe or an ISP that provides a complete automated installation package, you don't need to read this section – you're all set to go.)

Before you start to configure your computer, make sure that the modem is connected to the computer and telephone socket and switched on. Your ISP will have sent you a list of local phone numbers (called POPs – point of presence) that your modem uses to access the Internet. You also need your pre-assigned email address and the 'domain name' of the ISP computer. The domain name is a series of numbers that uniquely identifies every main computer on the Internet – it will look something like '198.122.22.3'. Once you've got these bits of information, you can configure your computer.

If computer-literate friends and children cannot get your system online, try the support line. But watch out – many free ISPs will charge heavily for this privilege.

Connecting a PC to the net Before you can connect to the Internet, you need to configure Microsoft Windows so that it knows how to access your ISP. The Windows software controls your PC and provides all the features you need to get on to the net – it also has a helpful Wizard that takes you step-by-step through the process of entering the information you need to configure your computer. If you are running an older version of Windows, such as 95 or even 3.x, you'll need to follow some extra steps that are explained in the box on page 22.

Steps to configure your PC

After making sure you have the basic information from your ISP (see above), simply follow these steps to configure your PC:

1 Double-click on the Internet Connection Wizard icon on the left of the Desktop. If there's no icon visible, the Wizard icon could be in one of two possible places: first, click on the Start button and look in Programs/Accessories/ Communications; if it's not there, try Programs/Internet Explorer.

2 Once the Wizard starts, it displays a welcome screen. Click on the Next button to move through the configuration steps.

3 The Wizard asks what type of new connection you want to create – choose the middle of the three options to set up this computer to access your own ISP.

4 Make sure that your modem is plugged in and switched on; click on the Next button and the Wizard will automatically dial Microsoft and display a list of the ISPs for which it carries details.

5 Choose your ISP from the list and click on the Next button. Windows will automatically retrieve almost all the configuration information required to connect to this ISP – you'll only need to type in your user name, password and email address.

6 If your ISP is not on the list, go back to step 3 and select the last of the three options to configure Windows manually. You'll have to follow a series of steps and type in the telephone number used to access the ISP, then the configuration settings provided by the ISP, together with your user name, password and email address.

7 You'll also be asked to configure the way in which you read electronic mail and access newsgroups. For these steps, you'll need the name of the mail servers used to send and receive message (these are sometimes called the SMTP and POP3 servers): their names will look like 'smtp.virgin.net' and 'pop.virgin.net'. To access newsgroups, you'll need the similar name for the newsgroup server (also called the NNTP server): it will look like 'news.virgin.net'.

8 Once you have entered the information, it is stored in a profile within the Dial-up Networking folder in the My Computer icon – just in case you need to make any changes.

Now that you have configured Windows, you can connect to the Internet and use your web browser or send and receive email messages. The Connection Wizard will have configured your computer so that when you run a web browser, it automatically dials and connects to the Internet. If, for some reason, you find that this doesn't happen automatically, double-click on the My

Computer icon, open the Dial-up Networking folder and double-click on your connection profile, which you created in the previous steps. This will connect you to the net.

Connecting a Macintosh to the net Before you can connect to the Internet, you need to configure your Macintosh so that it can access your ISP. If you have a new Macintosh that's running System 8 or 9, you'll get plenty of help from the Internet Setup Assistant. It takes you step-by-step through the process of configuring your Mac ready for the net. If you have an older machine, look to the box on page 22.

Steps to configure your Mac

After making sure you have the basic information from your ISP (see above), simply follow these steps to configure your Mac:

1 Double-click on the Internet Setup Assistant icon (or choose the Internet Access option from the Apple menu, then select Internet Setup Assistant).

2 Click on the 'yes' option to set up a new Internet account.

3 You'll follow through a series of simple screens. Each asks you to enter one of the bits of information supplied by your ISP.

4 Once you've finished, your Mac is configured. You're ready to go online.

Now that you have configured your Macintosh, you can connect to the Internet and use your web browser or send and receive email messages. The Setup Assistant should have configured your computer so that when you run a web browser, it automatically dials and connects to the Internet. If you find that this doesn't happen automatically, choose the Remote Access Status option from the Apple menu to make the connection.

If you keep getting disconnected from the Internet, make sure that you've disabled the 'call waiting' feature on your phone and that someone upstairs isn't trying to dial out at the same time.

Am I connected yet? If you double-click on the web browser icon on your Desktop, this will automatically start the Windows program that dials the ISP's access number and connects your computer to their bigger computer, which provides the doorway to the Internet. First of all, you'll see the Dialer warn you it's trying to dial the ISP's access number. Once it's connected, the Dialer window disappears and the web browser window appears. You're now connected to the net – you're online.

When you're online, Windows 98 displays a tiny icon in the bottom right-hand corner of the screen (next to the time) with two linked, tiny green squares. If you see this, you're online. The squares should flash bright green to show information is being transferred. The top square is the distant computer at the ISP and the bottom square represents your computer.

The first web page you'll see is either the Microsoft or Netscape welcome page (depending on the web browser you're using). Take a look somewhere else – for example, here's how to visit our page:

1 Move your mouse pointer to the address field (labelled 'Address') near the top left-hand corner of the browser.

2 Click once and the text in the field is highlighted. Start typing in a new web address – type in '**www.virgin-books.com**'. Press the Enter key.

3 Look in the bottom left-hand corner of your web browser – this is where you're told what is happening. First, the browser tells you it's trying to find this website, then it tells you it's trying to connect. After a second or two, you'll see our home page displayed. Welcome!

Your best support channel is that geeky friend who's really keen on his computer. Just make sure he really does know what he's talking about.

Trouble getting online? If you're having problems getting online, here are some of the common gremlins that beset new users:

1 When you start your web browser, does a window pop up (called the Dialer) to tell you the software is dialling and trying to connect to the net? If not, connect manually (see the 'Steps to configure' sections above).

2 When the Dialer pops up, does it say 'Dialing'? If not, there's a problem with your modem or modem settings. Make sure the modem is plugged in and switched on.

3 If the Dialer tells you there's 'no answer', make sure that you entered the access telephone number correctly.

4 When the Dialer connects, it displays a message that it has connected. Next, it sends your user name and password. If you see 'Authorisation error' or similar, there's a problem with your user name or password – they are case-sensitive, so enter them carefully.

Connecting an older computer to the net

If you have a computer that uses Windows 3.x or a Macintosh that uses System 6 or earlier, it's rather more difficult to get online. It's not impossible, but you'll have to use older software that rather lacks the friendly touch of the latest Wizards and Assistants.

First, ask your ISP if they have a setup CD for your type of operating system. If they do, it'll save a lot of trouble. AOL and CompuServe also have versions of their custom software that runs on older computers. If your ISP can't supply a setup CD, you'll need to find the software elsewhere. The best place to look is on the front cover of Internet-related magazines in your newsagent. The CDs displayed here normally have a library of essential software that will help get you started.

If you are still having problems and your ISP can't help find suitable software, you have two choices. You could visit a local Internet café or your library and spend an hour searching a site such as CNET (**www.cnet.com**) or TUCOWS (**www.tucows.com**) for suitable software. As a last resort, you might have to consider upgrading your computer so that it can run one of the newer operating systems. If your computer has 16Mb or more of memory and a Pentium or PowerPC processor, you should be able to upgrade the main operating system to Windows 98 or System 8 (for PCs and Macs, respectively).

//START SURFING

Let's get online and start surfing. Start your web browser and it will automatically start the dialer program that dials the access number and connects you to the Internet. It normally takes just under a minute to connect to the net – the dialer tells you what stage it's got to.

Once you are connected, the web browser automatically displays a 'home page'. This will probably be your ISP's main page, or you might see Microsoft's impressive MSN site or Netscape's rather feeble Netcenter site. You don't have to stick with the pre-assigned 'home page' – it's easy to change your web browser so that it displays your favourite sports page, shopping site or newspaper.

Here's how to change your browser's home page:

1 Start your web browser, connect to the Internet and visit your favourite site.

2 With the main page of the site displayed, select the Tools/Internet Options menu in IE or Edit/Preferences in Navigator.

3 A new dialog box is displayed and, near the top, there is a field with the site address of the current home page. Click on the button 'Use Current Page' to automatically insert the current site address.

4 Click on the OK button to confirm. Now, each time you start your browser, it displays your favourite page.

Visiting a site Just under the menu bar in the top left-hand corner is the Address window where you type in the URL for the website you want to visit. Click in the window and type in the address of the site you want to visit – for example, '**www.bbc.co.uk**' for the BBC's excellent website. You don't need to type in the initial 'http://' bit of an address – the browser fills this in for you. Press Return and the web browser tries to find and display the page. If it cannot find the site or page, you'll see an error message. If so, check you have typed in the address correctly and try again.

Some sites display extra pop-up windows in addition to your main web browser program. These are normally used to show advertising and can be very irritating. Close the windows to make sure you don't get a cluttered screen.

Surfing The main area of the web browser displays the web page. Hyperlinks normally appear on the page as underlined text. As you move your pointer over a link you'll see it change to a pointing-hand icon. Click and you'll jump to a new page.

You can display several separate copies of the browser window (each is called an instance) by pressing Ctrl-N (or Apple-N on a Mac). Each window works independently, so you can view separate sites or pages in each – use this tip to view the index page in one window and specific product details in another.

One extra tip that's particularly useful when using a search engine is to press down the Shift key when you click on a link. This opens the new page in a new browser window – it's an ideal way of keeping search results in one window while you're checking out the site in another. If you don't use this time-saver, you'll have to click the Back button to flip back to the search results.

//START EMAILING

To send or receive electronic mail messages, you need an email program and an Internet connection. The easiest way to start is to use the email software that's supplied with the web browsers from Microsoft or Netscape. If you used the Windows Wizard or Macintosh Assistant to help you set up your Internet connection, you will have been given the option to configure your email program. If you didn't, see below for the manual option.

Choosing an email address When you sign up with an ISP you'll be asked to choose an email address that will be unique to you and used by your friends to send you messages. (The only exception is

CompuServe, which assigns you a number. However, you can change this to a word or name that's easier to remember by typing 'go name'.)

When you choose your email address, you'll probably type in your first name and your surname. For example, if you're signing up for Freeserve, you might type in 'john@smith.freeserve.net'. Unfortunately, because of the huge number of other subscribers, you can be pretty certain that your name has already been assigned to someone else. The ISP will suggest an available address, like 'john@smith72.freeserve.net'. If you don't mind the number, fine. However, why not try a few alternatives to get a really unique address. You could try 'john@smith_family.freeserve.net' or, as you get more desperate for a unique name, even your hobby, nickname or house name.

Your email address only really matters the first time you tell a friend. From then on, they can add you to their email address book and send you a message by selecting the entry from the address book list. If you send someone an email message, almost all email programs let the recipient right-click on the message to automatically add the sender to their address book.

If you're setting up different addresses for each member of the family, make sure that you pick a provider that offers multiple email addresses – for everyone in the gang. The simplest solution is to use the Windows Profiles feature to create totally separate views of Windows, email and browsing for each member of the family. Open the Start/Settings/ Control Panel window and double-click on the Users icon.

Setting up your email program If you are running the installation software from your ISP, or if you used the automatic Wizard or Assistant to configure your Internet connection (see earlier in this chapter), then you will be asked to type in the email address you've chosen and a password. Once you've done this, your email program will automatically configure the email program for you – you're now ready to send and receive messages.

To check if everything works, ask the email program to check if there is any new mail. It should start the Dialer automatically, connect to the Internet and contact the post office server. If you get to this stage and you see an error message, you've entered either the wrong address for the post office or the wrong name and/or password. Check all three and try again.

The manual option

If your ISP didn't supply a friendly installation program or you didn't use the Wizard or Assistant to do the hard work for you, you'll need to set up your email program yourself. It's not too difficult, with just a few steps. You'll find it easier to start by using the email program supplied with your web browser – you can always change later to a different program. The following steps will guide you through the manual set up process:

1 Open your web browser. To start the email program, choose the Go/Mail menu option if you're using Microsoft's IE, or Communicator/Messenger Mailbox in Netscape. This starts a separate program: Microsoft Outlook Express or Netscape Messenger.

2 You need to open the setup screen: in Microsoft's Outlook Express, this is under Mail/Options; in Netscape Messenger, it's under the Edit/Preferences menu.

3 The program will ask you to enter your own email address and password (normally the same as your standard Internet password) and the names of the two email servers supplied by your ISP.

4 Once you have typed in all four pieces of information, you are ready to send and receive messages.

You can test your email connection by sending us a message – we'll send a reply straight back! Type in the 'To' address as 'test@virgin-pub.com' and click on the Send button, then the Send/Receive button. The email software will connect to the Internet and send the message. Wait a minute or two and then click on Send/Receive again to pick up any new mail.

How email works

When you want to send a message, the email program contacts a special computer – a server – at your ISP called the post office. You'll need the address of this post office (often called an SMTP or mail server). When you're ready to read any new messages, your email program contacts a different post office server that's called a POP server. Some ISPs combine both functions into one address but generally they are on different servers. For example, if you use Virgin Net in the UK then the post office server responsible for sending mail is at 'smtp.virgin.net' and the server you need to contact when reading mail is at 'pop.virgin.net'. This combination of POP and SMTP is rather old-fashioned. The newest standard, IMAP4, is just starting to gain wide support but, for the moment, you don't need to change.

//USING NEWSGROUPS

There are tens of thousands of individual newsgroups, each providing a discussion forum for a particular subject. They work rather like a noticeboard – anyone can post a message that can then be read by any other user.

Newsgroups are one of the most active areas of the Internet. To join in, you'll need special software called a newsgroup reader, which lets you read notices and submit your own, and a normal connection to the Internet.

Both Microsoft and Netscape include a newsgroup reader with their free web browser programs – there are alternative programs that you can download from the web, but the built-in readers are a great way to get started. If you used a special setup CD-ROM from your ISP or configured your web browser using the setup Wizard or Assistant, it's almost certain that your newsgroup reader is ready to use. If not, see the box on how to configure your software. Here's how to use your software:

1 If you use Microsoft's IE web browser, the newsgroup reader is part of the email program, Outlook Express. Start this by choosing the Tools/Mail&News/Read News menu option. In Netscape's browser, you'll need to start the Messenger email program (Communicator/Messenger) and then click on the news server listed in the left-hand pane. No, they don't make it easy!

2 On the left-hand side of either program is a list of icons – at the bottom of this list should be an entry that starts with the word 'news'. For example, if you subscribe to the Demon Internet ISP, it would read 'news.virgin.net'. If there's no entry, see the box on how to configure your newsgroup reader, which also explains how to add a newsgroup server.

3 In Microsoft Outlook, double-click on this icon (in Netscape, right-click and choose the 'Subscribe to newsgroups' option).

4 The software will automatically dial up and connect to the Internet. It then downloads a list of all the newsgroups

currently available – this could take several minutes. Finally, you'll see the list displayed.

5 Click on any item from the list (or type in a word to narrow the list to those newsgroups that include this word) and click on the Subscribe button.

6 The screen changes to show the latest notices that have been posted to the newsgroup.

How to configure your newsgroup reader

Setting up your newsgroup reader software is very similar to setting up email software. You will need the name of the special computer that your ISP uses to store all the newsgroup messages (called the newsgroup server). This should be in your welcome pack. You will also need your normal Internet user name and password. Follow these steps:

1 Start the newsgroup reader program (Outlook Express or Messenger). The first time you start the software, it should ask you to type in the name of the newsgroup server, your user name and password.

2 If the software does not ask you for this information, you'll need to find the setup screen. In Netscape, select the Edit/Preferences menu option and choose the Mail & Groups/Groups Server option from the list on the left-hand side. In Microsoft, choose the Tools/Accounts menu option and click on the News page tab. Click on the Add button on the right-hand side.

3 Type in the name of the newsgroup server, as supplied by your ISP. It should start with the word 'news' and will look something like 'news.demon.co.uk' (for Demon ISP users).

4 Click on OK and the software will add this newsgroup server as an icon at the bottom of the list displayed on the left-hand side of the software.

//SETTING UP IRC (INTERNET RELAY CHAT)

IRC lets you type in a message that's seen instantly by any other user in the discussion group (called a channel). You need special software to use IRC to let you view the message – the chat – typed in by you and the other users. Unlike newsgroups, this all happens live and in front of a small audience (if you want a one-to-one chat, try instant messaging – see later).

For a quick and fun way to try out chat, use Microsoft Chat, which is part of the Internet Explorer web browser (you'll find the program in Start/Programs/Internet Explorer). Type in your nickname, email address and choose a comic character from this list – then join in the chat!

Get chatting with IRC To use IRC, you'll need a standard Internet connection and some special IRC software – you don't need a web browser or email program. Unusually, IRC software (normally called the client) is not bundled in as part of either the Microsoft or Netscape web browsers.

If you received a CD-ROM starter pack from your ISP, there's sure to be an IRC client on there. If not, download a version: the most popular PC program is mIRC (free from **www.mirc.com**) and for the Mac it's IRCle (from **www.ircle.com**) or ChatNet (from **www.elsinc.com**).

Here's how to get started with IRC:

1 Install an IRC client program (or download the program, then install it).

2 You'll be prompted to type in your nickname and email address – type in a name you want to use as a nickname (it's displayed to other users in the channel), your real name and your normal email address. Some IRC servers check that your email address is correct and will refuse you entry if you enter a fake.

3 You need to enter the name of a computer that allows chatting – the software will have a list of friendly computers (called 'IRC chat servers'). Choose one from the File menu list. (Alternatively, your ISP might host an IRC chat server that will have local users or visit Liszt (**www.liszt.com**), which has a database of independent IRC chat servers).

4 When you choose the chat server, your software connects to the server and displays a list of the various discussion groups available at the moment (called channels).

5 Choose one of the channels from the list and you'll enter the group and see the chat messages from other users in the group.

Once you have selected a channel, you'll see the messages from other members displayed in one part of the screen – the other sections of the screen show the list of channels and the nicknames of the users in this channel. To start with, just spend a couple of minutes reading the conversations. It can be rather daunting to leap in without an introduction, but stick with it – it's great fun.

//INSTANT MESSAGING

Instant messaging (IM) has rapidly become one of the most popular ways of chatting to other users. You can decide if you want to have a private chat with a friend or enter a free-for-all session with a group of strangers. Best of all, you can configure IM so that it alerts you when a friend or colleague is online and ready to chat.

Setting it up To start chatting with instant messaging, you'll need some special software and a connection to the Internet. Unlike IRC and newsgroups, each type of IM software uses a different system of sending messages so, generally, they are incompatible. Although there are dozens of different programs available, three dominate. ICQ, AOL and Yahoo! Pager have the largest number of users and are easy to use. If you use the latest Netscape browser or subscribe to AOL, you are already set up to use AOL Instant Messaging. If you are with another ISP, you'll have to download one of the special software systems, but it's free.

One of the benefits of instant messaging is that the better systems include a directory of users, making it relatively easy to locate a friend or colleague for a chat. However, this means that you'll have to enter more information to configure the software – and your entry in the directory. Here's how to set it up and get going:

1 Decide if you want to try AOL, ICQ or Yahoo! Pager. Or you can try each – first download the software from AOL (**www.aol.co.uk/aim**), ICQ (**www.icq.com**) or Yahoo! (**www.yahoo.com**).

2 Install the software on your computer. The program will ask you to type in your real name, nickname, email address and (optionally) a description of yourself or your interests.

3 Next, you need to set up the level of privacy you want to use – do you want to allow any other user to call you for a chat or do you want to restrict this list to just a few known friends?

4 Lastly, start the software and connect to the Internet.

The chat software will sit quietly in the background while you surf with your web browser or check your email – until another user asks you if you want to chat. It will then pop up and tell you who's calling and give you the option to start a conversation.

//ADDRESS BOOK

Major ISPs

This modest range of ISPs comprises some of the larger companies that have been providing Internet access for several years. There are hundreds of other ISPs – some small, local companies, others offering national coverage. These companies will set you up with an account for a monthly payment; each provides basic dial-up access for users with modems but can scale up to businesses with high-speed ISDN links or specialist requirements.

AOL **www.aol.com**
0800 376 5432

BT Internet **www.btinternet.com**
0800 800 001

CompuServe **www.compuserve.com**
0990 000 200

Demon **www.demon.net**
0845 272 2666

Direct Connection **www.dircon.net**
0800 072 0000

Easynet **www.easynet.net**
0845 333 4000

Global Internet **www.global.net.uk**
0870 909 8042

IBM **www.ibm.net**
0990 426 426

Netcom **www.netcom.net.uk**
0990 668080

Uunet **www.uunet.co.uk**
0845 0884455

Free ISPs

Getting in touch with free ISPs by phone is hard work – they only like to give out premium rate support lines. For BTClick, call the operator and ask BT to send a CD; for Freeserve, visit Dixons or PC World; X-stream and LineOne expect you to download their software from their websites; Virgin Net lets you sign up online, or they will send you a welcome pack and CD.

BT Click	**www.btclick.com**
LineOne	**www.lineone.net**
Virgin Net	**www.virgin.net**
Freeserve	**www.freeserve.co.uk**
Netscape Online	**www.netscapeonline.co.uk**
X-stream	**www.x-stream.co.uk**

2//SURFING FOR SHOPPERS

Nobody needs to be taught how to shop – indeed, given the enthusiasm displayed by many shoppers, some would say it's an innate ability, perhaps even a God-given talent. However, the way Internet-based shops work and the mechanical process of choosing and paying for goods is rather different to the high-street version you're used to. In this chapter, you'll find out how to use the different types of shop – from auction to classifieds – and the different ways to order and pay for items.

//HOW TO SHOP

There are four basic ways of shopping on the net. These provide different ways of choosing the item, paying for it and getting it delivered. You'll see all four in action as you browse shops online.

Shopping carts

Any shop that lets you order and pay for goods online now provides an electronic shopping cart. As you browse or search the site, you'll see each item has a 'Buy Me' button beside it – look at Amazon (**www.amazon.co.uk**) as an example. Click on the button and the item is added to your virtual basket.

When you've finished and want to pay, click on the 'Checkout' button (it will be somewhere prominent: the shop doesn't want to lose your sale). The site displays a list of the items in your shopping cart; you can still remove items or change the quantities. Click on the 'Proceed' or 'Order' button and you will move to a secure web page (your browser displays a closed padlock icon in the bottom status bar to confirm this). Here, you will be asked to fill in your delivery and credit card details. Finally, the site will ask how you want the items to be delivered – there's normally a range of regular, fast or courier delivery options. Don't enter any personal or credit card information unless you see the closed padlock icon.

And so to the last step: you will see a full summary of all the charges, plus delivery and any local VAT or other taxes. Click on the 'Purchase' or 'Proceed' button and the order will be finalised. You can cancel the order at any time until this final click. Now, you will see an order reference that you should note down. The most sophisticated sites let you revisit at any time, type in your order number and check on its progress – use this order-tracking feature to make sure the items aren't lost in the post.

The items that you've bought will either be sent to you by courier or mail, or you will get instant access – see the section covering virtual consumption, below.

Requirements To buy with a shopping cart, you should use a browser that supports one of the secure website standards (see the chapter on security for more details). In practice, this means support for the SSL standard that's provided by the latest versions of Netscape and Microsoft browsers. If your current browser doesn't support SSL then we strongly recommend that you upgrade before you shop. Check that your browser supports SSL by visiting VeriSign (**www.verisign.com**) and using their online test.

Most shops implement their carts using software on the distant server computer. However, some shopping carts use a special plug-in or applet that runs on your computer. If the site uses this system, your browser will automatically download the software the first time you shop there. One applet that's commonly used is called Shop@ssistant and it takes around 20–30 seconds to download. When you're shopping, there's no difference between different types of cart – it's just a matter of choice for the shop designer.

Auctions

Auctions are one of the best ways to find cheap, antique or collectable items. One person (or company) advertises an item and any visitor can place a bid. After a certain period of time (normally a week), the auction stops and the highest bid wins.

Auction sites do not generally deal with your money. Instead, you register your personal details (name, address and email) then you can start to place bids on items advertised for auction. All the business of paying for the item, shipping, guarantees and complaints are between you and the vendor – and normally worked out by sending emails.

If yours is the winning bid, you will need to send the money to the vendor within a few days, either by draft or direct transfer. This is arranged directly with the vendor (although there are some companies that will manage this for you – see page 74 under 'Payments'). The whole system works on trust, not credit cards. As a result, it's one of the best places to find scams and crooks. Turn to Chapter 6 for a full guide to using auctions safely.

Requirements You only need a browser and an Internet connection to bid at an auction. You pay the vendor directly, so there are no special requirements for security.

Classified ads

Online classifieds are just the same as those in a local paper or magazine. You're using the web to help you find the classified ad that details your dream car, washing machine or whatever. Once you've found the ad, you'll have to email or phone the vendor to get further details and arrange to haggle and buy. Most of the major classified-ad weekly papers are online and let you search through the entire paper in an instant. The three best known sites are: *AutoTrader* (**www.autotrader.co.uk**), *Exchange and Mart* (www.exchangeandmart.co.uk) and *Loot* (www.loot.co.uk).

Requirements To search the big classified sites, such as *Exchange and Mart*, you need a browser and an Internet connection. If you want to look for ads in newsgroups, use a newsgroup reader (this software is built into the latest crop of web browsers) or use the Deja.com site (www.deja.com).

Virtual consumption

So far, all of the different types of shop and ways of shopping have the same basic product: it's something visible, physical and deliverable. If you want to buy a book or a shirt, a coffee cup or a necklace, you are seeing and paying for a real 'thing'.

It's fitting that this virtual world allows virtual consumption. These are shops and outlets that let you buy products or information that is consumed online or fed directly to your computer.

There are many different types of shop that provide virtual consumption. The sex industry is certainly the most prolific in this area. Currently, roughly 10% of all online business is conducted in a virtual sex store – imagine that on your high street! Some organisations charge for subscription to their site, which then lets you see pictures and read stories; others charge to view videos directly on your browser. You pay by credit card and are charged as you use the service. However much you may despise the sex industry, it has been almost solely responsible for driving forward the revolution in online shopping (and the entire multimedia experience) that you're now enjoying in other, rather less exotic, shops.

Aside from the sex, there are plenty of other benign sites that let you buy and consume directly. If you want to buy a software application, you can order the shrink-wrapped boxed package from a normal online shop like Action (www.action.co.uk) or

Inmac (**www.inmac.co.uk**) and it will be posted to you. Alternatively, you can visit the developer's site or a direct sales operation like Download (**www.download.com**), pay a reduced price and download the software application directly to your computer. It's 'instant' and cheaper – although it can take an age to download.

Working with a similar sales model, music is now also available to download, providing instant playback. The CD-quality music is stored in a standard file format (the most commonly used is called MP3): you visit the shop, choose the album, pay a reduced price, download the MP3 file and you have the complete, original (and legal) version of your favourite album. You can play this on your computer or buy a Walkman-style portable player and transfer the file to this.

Other sites include those that charge a subscription to read or access information – for example the Economist Intelligence Unit (**www.eiu.com**) will charge for full access to its archives of business reports. At the other, arty, end of the site spectrum, you can pay for a virtual ticket, then watch a classic European film on your browser at Eurocinema (**www.eurocinema.com**).

//USING THE WEB

All the shops on the Internet are part of the web and so, to shop online, you'll need to use a web browser. Shops can be in a site dedicated to the buying experience or part of an existing site that combines other information with the chance to spend money. A website is a collection of web pages that stands on its own; for example, the Microsoft website (**www.microsoft.com**) has thousands of pages about all the products in the Gates empire. Each site has a home page – it's the first page that's displayed when you visit the site. The home page is almost always stored in a file called 'index.html'. If you type in a website address without a specific web page, you'll see the home page. Visit '**www.bbc.co.uk**' or '**www.bbc.co.uk/index.html**' and you'll see the same page.

Each page file has a name and it usually ends with the file extension 'html' – like 'news.html'. Sometimes, pages have an 'htm' extension – but it means the same thing. If you see a page ending 'asp' (for example 'news.asp') then you're seeing a site that uses ASP (active server page) to create the page only just before it is displayed. You cannot normally reference an 'asp' page directly; if you try, you'll almost certainly see a warning message that the page has expired. Large online shops often produce their individual product pages using ASP, so it can be hard to bookmark the page.

Ever wonder why the mega shopping sites slow down? They have to combine fast database access (to search their inventory) with links to the credit card companies (to clear payments) – for hundreds of thousands of visitors per day.

Sites to beware You need to be vigilant when shopping on the net to be sure you're dealing with a reputable company. Sometimes you'll see an address like 'www.compuserve.com/simon/'. This is an example of a small, individual site located in an all-encompassing larger domain. It's still a website with its own collection of web pages and it is totally different from 'www. compuserve.com/fred/'. These types of address are very common in smaller, enthusiast-run sites. Two of the biggest umbrella domains for small sites are GeoCities (**www.geocities.com**) and Tripod (**www.tripod.com**) – they provide free web space and let anyone create their own site.

When shopping, avoid online shops that are based on a free web service. Sounds harsh, but it's likely it's either a scam or you'll simply have huge problems in the event of a complaint. If the company or person cannot be bothered – or afford – to fork out the £50 to register a domain, they are unlikely to bother supplying your order. There are enough alternatives to ensure that you'll still find what you need. Unfortunately, there are some sites that might seem fine, but aren't. For full details on how to avoid being tricked and duped by online shops, flip to Chapter 4.

Web browsers

To surf and view web pages you'll need a web browser. Its job is simply to decode the HTML instructions in a web page file and display the formatted results on screen.

There are two main contenders that dominate the browser market: Microsoft's Internet Explorer and Netscape's Navigator. Each company tries to introduce new technological trickery that will improve the web – and foil its rival. Both have leapfrogged each other over the years so now there's little difference between the two. And there's no price difference either – both are free (you'll find them on the CDs on the front of computer magazines or download the latest version from **www.microsoft.com** and **www.netscape.com**) and both run on PCs and Macs.

The best advice is try them both and stick with the one you like best. If you're using a PC then the latest IE (version 5) probably has the edge. Macintosh users will find the Netscape browser more advanced than Microsoft's offering.

Using your web browser

Start your web browser and it automatically starts the Dialer that connects you to the Internet. The browser finds and displays your designated 'home page'. Your web browser will probably display your ISP's home page or possibly the home page for Microsoft or Netscape. It's worth changing your home page to your favourite site – if you're a dedicated shopper, set your browser's home page to a site that lists the day's top deals, such as ShopSmart (**www.shopsmart.com**) or a specialist shop like Amazon (**www.amazon.co.uk**). See page 24 for details of how to do this.

Navigating There are several different ways of moving (surfing) from one website or page to another:

- Move to a new site or page by typing in the address in the Address window in the top left corner.
- Jump from one page to another by clicking on links in the page.
- Move back through the previous pages that you visited in this session by clicking on the 'Back' arrow in the button bar.

Visiting a site Just under the menu bar in the top left-hand corner is the Address window where you type in the URL for the website you want to visit. Click in the window and type in the address of the site you want to visit – for example '**www.bbc.co.uk**' for the BBC's excellent website. You don't need to type in the initial 'http://' bit of an address – the browser fills this in for you. Once you have typed in the address, press Return on your keyboard and the web browser tries to find and display the page. If it cannot find the site or page, you'll see an error message. If so, check you have typed in the address correctly and try again (see Chapter 3 for more information on finding websites).

//SURFING

The main area of the web browser window displays the web page. You'll see the text and layout defined according to the HTML instructions in the page. Hyperlinks normally appear on the page as underlined text. As you move your pointer over a link you'll see it change to a pointing-hand icon. Click once and you'll jump to a new page.

You can display several separate copies of the browser window by pressing Ctrl-N (or Apple-N on a Mac). Each window works independently, so you can view separate sites or pages in each – use this tip to view share prices in one window while you browse sports results in another.

One extra tip that's particularly useful when using a search engine is to press down the Shift key when you click on a link. This opens the new page in a new browser window – it's an ideal way of keeping search results in one window while you're checking out the site in another. If you don't use this time-saver, you'll have to click the Back button to flip back to the search results.

Keep track of your favourite sites If you visit a site or page you're likely to visit again, you can bookmark it. To add a bookmark, press Ctrl-B (in IE) or Ctrl-D (in Navigator) or choose the Favourites menu option (in IE) or the Communicator/Bookmarks menu option (in Navigator).

To revisit a site that you have bookmarked, simply display the list of bookmarks (using the Communicator/Bookmarks or Favourites menu option) and click on its entry from the list. As you start to create more bookmarks, you can create convenient folders and use these to organise the bookmarks into different categories. For example, you could create a folder for financial, another for food and a third for e-zines.

To help manage and organise your bookmarks simply follow these steps and create a new folder:

1 In Navigator, choose the Communicator/Bookmarks menu option; in IE, click on the Favourites menu option.

2 Select the Edit Bookmarks option from Navigator or the Organize Favourites option in IE.

3 You'll see a list of the folders that are supplied with the browser. Click on the File/New Folder menu option in Navigator or click on the Create Folder button in IE.

4 Finally, type in a name for your new folder and add a descriptive comment.

When you add a new bookmark, you might be asked if you want to subscribe to this site. This only happens if the site designer has provided support for this advanced option. Choose 'yes' and you will be informed whenever the page changes. This is great if you want to keep up to date with a company's news or software updates.

Stopping an action Sometimes the browser might seem to freeze. This is normally because the Internet is busy or it cannot find a site – or the site is overloaded and taking ages to reply. Time is precious, so stop the browser waiting for a reply by clicking on the Stop icon in the button bar at the top of the window.

If the browser appears to freeze when you have just submitted an order – don't stop the action! For example, if you have just placed an order, the order-processing computer will need to check the order and, probably, verify your credit card details. It can take from 10 – 60 seconds to process everything – so be patient.

Security If you're about to type in any important personal or financial information at a website – such as your credit card number when paying for shopping – make sure you are aware of security. The Internet was not designed to transfer private, personal information; if you send anything over the Internet, it is transferred in its plain, readable form. The upshot of this is that if a hacker is tapping your phone line, he or she could read whatever you send or receive. Sounds awful, but in practice it's pretty hard to do and not worth the bother from the hacker's point of view.

If you want to send credit card details and other personal information over the Internet, it's important that this information is not sent in plain, readable form. The lure of a credit card number makes it rather more worthwhile for a hacker to get to work.

To counter this threat, there are two solutions: one, make sure that any important information is sent in an encrypted, scrambled form or, two, make sure that hackers cannot gain access to the net. The second is almost impossible but, in an attempt to achieve this, secure websites have been developed, which provide a secure channel between your browser and the website.

When you visit a secure website, the web server sends a signal to your web browser to ask it to switch to secure mode. The browser and server exchange security details, then establish a secure link – any information transferred between the browser and the server is now scrambled using a resilient method of encryption. A determined hacker can still intercept the information you are sending to the website but, since it's encrypted, he or she can't read it.

Only type in your credit card details or other personal information when you see the closed padlock icon in the bottom line of your web browser

---

When your browser has established a secure channel, a tiny closed padlock icon is displayed in the status bar at the bottom of the browser window. All the new, current versions of web browsers support SSL. If you have an older version of a browser, or just want to check everything is working, visit the VeriSign site (**http://**

www.verisign.com) and use the online test that tells you if your browser is SSL-compatible.

There are new security systems being developed – notably SET – and you'll find these filtering their way into the various software packages and websites over the next year. (For more details on the issue of online security, refer to Chapter 4.)

Printing pages If you've just placed an order, the shopping system should confirm the order and display an order code and, often, customer enquiry numbers or a link to monitor your order. You should print this page to keep a record of your order. Choose the File/Print menu option or click on the Printer icon on the button bar of your browser. If the page uses frames for layout, the print options window will ask which frame of the page you want to display. To get something that looks just like the original on screen, choose the 'As Laid Out on Screen' option.

Cookies

Forget Rich Tea – a cookie is a scrap of information stored by a website on your hard disk. It's stored in a special file and enables the website to keep track of your favourite options, when you last visited the site and your personal tastes. The more sophisticated shops use cookies to keep track of what's in your shopping cart. It's a way of helping you – for example, if you lose your connection, revisit the shop and you'll find the basket still full of the products you had selected.

Most of the major shopping sites ask new customers to register before they place an order. You'll be asked for your email address, name and – usually – a password. Your name and your favourite shopping decisions (fiction/non-fiction, organic/non-organic, window seat/aisle and so on) might all be stored in cookies on your computer. Similarly, if you customise the portal sites, such as Excite!

(www.excite.co.uk) or MSN (www.msn.com), your choices are stored as cookies. Next time you visit the site, it will probably welcome you by name. Generally, there's nothing dangerous about cookies, but it can be disconcerting to visit a site and be welcomed with 'Back again? You were only here yesterday evening.' Most sites only use cookies to keep track of your visits and your custom options – giving them valuable marketing information that helps tailor their site.

Many of the newer shopping-cart systems won't work if you have switched off support for cookies in your browser.

To see what's stored about you (on your own computer) by other people, you can see the cookies registered on your computer: for example, in IE, choose the View/Internet Options menu option, then choose the Settings button in the Temporary Internet Files section of the General page tag.

Downloading files

One of the most popular items sold on the net is software. You pay for a product, at a discount price, then download the software directly on to your computer – saving time, money and shipping charges. There are two ways to download files on to your computer. Most large commercial sites display details of the file together with a hyperlink to the file; click on the link and your browser automatically starts to download the file. The browser displays a dialog box giving you the option to save the file on to your hard disk or run the file. Select the save option and the file will start to be transferred on to your computer.

Handling compressed files

Most files are compressed before they are stored on the Internet ready for you to download – this saves download time. You can double-click on a PC file that ends in 'EXE' or a Mac file that ends 'SEA' and they will automatically decompress themselves without any extra software. If the filename ends with the letters 'ZIP' (for PCs) or 'HQX' or 'SIT' (for Macs) you'll need an unzip utility to decompress the program. The most popular is WinZip **(www.winzip.com)** but you'll find alternatives at Filez (**www.filez.com**) or CNET (**www.cnet.com**).

FTP servers If a computer is dedicated to storing files ready for you to download, it's called an FTP server. A good example is **www.shareware.com** that stores hundreds of thousands of shareware programs.

If you visit a website that lets you download a file, your web browser can manage the the entire process. Click on a hyperlink that says 'download me' and your browser will automatically talk to the FTP server and transfer the file.

Some FTP servers run in a protected environment, and so require a password – you'll be prompted to enter a user ID and password. Most FTP servers allow guests to enter and download files by logging in as an anonymous user. Type in 'anonymous' as a user ID and your email address as the password and you should see a listing of the folders and files available to download.

For users who plan to do a lot of file transfers, or visit academic sites (which mostly still use FTP servers with anonymous login), you'll find life easier with an FTP client program. These are all shareware or freeware. Visit CNET (**www.cnet.com**) or Filez (**www.filez.com**) and search for FTP – you'll get a list of the latest versions of the top clients. Click on a link and let your browser download the program.

Whenever you download a file, scan it with a virus detector before you run it. One of the most popular virus detection programs is by McAfee (**www.mcafee.com**).

Watching films, playing music

You'll encounter music and video clips on many of the sites you visit, for example the fabulous All-Music Guide (**www.allmusic.com**), where you can listen to music clips and watch video segments from thousands of bands.

Most music and video websites are funded by their sales of CDs or videotapes, but you can also buy sound files or watch a video online with direct delivery to your computer. For example, if you've got a sudden urge to listen to Louis Armstrong or The Verve, visit one of the sites that sells sound files in the new standard MP3 format. Buy the file, download it and play it back in full glorious stereo either via your browser or in a special MP3 player (there are several tiny players on the market).

If you want to watch a video, you could order the tape and wait for it to be delivered – or you can pay and watch a video on your screen. Admittedly, most of the sites offering this are porn-based, but you could watch an art-based or obscure black and white film from one of the virtual cinemas (such as Eurocinema – **www.eurocinema.com**). Once you have bought a virtual ticket, you can watch the film through your browser.

The newest web browsers include support for most standard ways of transferring music, video and animation over the web, so just sit back and enjoy. If your browser doesn't support the standard then you'll see a warning message that asks if you want to download a plug-in to add support to your browser.

Before the download starts, you should see a certificate displayed telling you about the company that developed the plug-in – only continue with the download if you have heard of the company (or it's one of the companies in the list below). The download and installation is automatic and your newly enhanced browser will be able to play back multimedia clips stored in this particular format (multimedia and animation sites normally use the Shockwave plug-in, which can be downloaded from **www.macromedia.com**).

There are two ways of making music available on the net. Either copy the music to a file and let users download the file to play on their computers (this technique is used by MP3 and WAV files) or wait till the user asks to play the music, then play it back, live, over the Internet connection (as with Real). The latest versions of Microsoft and Netscape browsers include software that can relay these formats automatically. Alternatively, you can download special dedicated software that gives you more control over the way the music is played.

The best sites to find MP3 files and information are:

MP3.com	**www.mp3.com**
Lycos Music	**http://mp3.lycos.com**
MP3.dk	**www.mp3.dk**

And the following provide information on alternative music formats:

Real	**www.real.com**
WinAmp	**www.winamp.com**

Speeding up your browsing

You might find it hard to believe, but your computer does not automatically provide the most efficient settings for browsing the

Internet. There is plenty of scope to improve performance by tweaking some of the settings. The problem is, you'll need to adjust the TCP/IP and internal Windows settings – and they are rather complicated to tackle.

Dozens of utility programs are now available that promise to boost your Internet access performance just by adjusting these hidden settings. Some work well, others don't. It doesn't help that the goalposts keep moving as Microsoft and the other developers of these utilities each try to improve performance. Before you spend your money on wild promises, take a look at the CNET (**www.cnet.com**) and Zdnet (**www.zdnet.com**) sites and read the latest reviews and benchtest figures for the current crop of utilities.

Browsing offline

There was a vogue for browsing websites offline, to save on connection charges. However, as websites have become more complex and bigger, and Internet access charges have been slashed, it's not such a big issue.

It is relatively easy to view web pages even when you're not connected to the Internet. The first method uses the temporary files that your web browser stores on your hard disk as you browse. When you start your web browser, click on the Work Offline button from the Dialer utility to prevent it dialling out. Now type in the URL of a page you've visited recently and the browser should be able to display it. (The temporary files are only stored for a certain amount of time, so it might not be there.) If you try and view a page that's no longer in the temporary store (called the cache), the browser will attempt to dial up and connect to the Internet.

The second method is to use a specialist utility program that saunters up to a website and downloads the whole lot on to your hard disk. This was a fine idea when websites had just a few dozen pages, but try this on the CNN or BBC site and you'll wait around for days as the thousands of individual pages are downloaded. Once you have downloaded the site on to your drive, you can browse it as if you were online. The best-known of these utilities include Teleport (**www.tenmax.com**), UnMozify (**www.evolve.co.uk**), Insite (**www.engr.orst.edu**) and WebWhacker (**www.webwhacker.com**).

Protecting the kids

Because of its history as a forum for uncensored free speech, there's plenty of unpleasant material out in the big bad Internet – and most parents would rather that junior didn't find out about it just yet. When using the Internet for shopping, you also want to make sure your kids don't run riot with your credit card or more unauthorised bids at online auctions. There are several ways to prevent access to particular sites and newsgroups.

If you have a whole family of different users on your PC, Windows 98 includes a special feature (User Profiles) that lets each have their own individual browser, bookmarks and email settings. Switch it on from the Start/Settings/Control Panel/Users icon.

If you subscribe to AOL, you can use the Parental Control option to control which sites and newsgroups can be viewed by the other family accounts. Non-AOL surfers can either use a commercial program that can be set up to prevent access to a vast list of X-rated sites, or you can configure your browser yourself.

Commercial programs such as NetNanny (**www.netnanny.com**) and SurfWatch (**www.surfwatch.com**) provide a decent solution but won't be able to catch every site. Get a complete list of the programs available from **www.worldvillage.com/wv/school/html/control.htm**. If you want to do it yourself then use Microsoft's IE browser – it lets you bar content in various categories. Choose the Options/View/Security menu command and select which categories you want to block with the Content Advisor settings.

//ADDRESS BOOK

Web Browsers

The free software you need to view and surf web pages:

Microsoft **www.microsoft.com**
Netscape's deadly rival has its own market-leading web browser, Internet Explorer, which is free to download.

Netscape **www.netscape.com**
The Navigator web browser is now free to download.

Opera **www.opera.com**
The independent browser that is fast, full-featured and trails a cult following.

Offline Browsers

Save on phone bills with these handy utilities:

Teleport **www.tenmax.com**
UnMozify **www.evolve.co.uk**
WebWhacker **www.webwhacker.com**

Parental Control

Protect your children from the muck on the net with software to block access. AOL users get this built in.

CyberPatrol **www.cyberpatrol.com**
Keep the kids in the safe zone by installing this rival to NetNanny – set up restricted zones to prevent kids from visiting X-rated sites.

NetNanny **www.netnanny.com**
Top-selling utility that prevents your kids from visiting X-rated or anti-social websites and newsgroups.

SurfMonkey **www.surfmonkey.com**

Creates a neat, jolly and controlled environment with its own browser that restricts what kids can do and where they can visit.

SurfWatch **www.surfwatch.com**

Monitor and limit the areas your children visit on the net.

WorldVillage Parental Guide **www.worldvillage.com/wv/school/html/control.htm**

A complete guide to the products available for parental control.

3//SEARCHING

You know it's out there, but how do you find it? The Internet contains tens of thousands of shops that sell just about everything you could ever want to own. The trick is not just to find the shop that stocks the item, but to find the shop that sells the item at the cheapest price. In this chapter, we'll show you how to make best use of the directories, search engines and online assistants.

//LOOKING FOR THE BEST PRICE

To get the best price with the least effort, let specialist price-comparison websites do the work for you. These sites let you type in the name of a product, then they submit it to a range of online stores – and report back with the lowest prices. Most of the guides are limited to basic categories of product that are easy to compare (books, music, video, software, sports goods and computers), but it's a quick and convenient way to shop around.

The only problem is that although these are part of everyday surfing life in the United States, only a few have made it to the UK. Buy.co.uk (**www.buy.co.uk**) lets you compare prices of home utilities so you can find the cheapest electricity or gas. For consumer products, however, there are only a few that deal specifically with British shops – Shopgenie (**www.shopgenie.com**), ShopSmart (**www.shopsmart.com**) and Taxi (**www.mytaxi.co.uk**). At the moment they work across a limited range of goods such as books, CDs and videos.

Price-comparison websites are set up to check prices at a range of online shops: take a careful look at the selection process for these shops (which should be displayed in the About or Service page) – sometimes these are included because people have recommended them, sometimes they're here because of financial incentives (that means advertising!).

If you don't mind buying from overseas, you'll probably get a better price in the United States, but there are three points against you. First, shipping costs (which can treble the price of a book but are less significant if you're buying a computer); second, the manufacturer's warranty might not stretch outside the United States and, third, many online shops won't deal with international customers.

Price-comparison Sites

Find the best deal online with these special sites that let you compare the price of the same item as sold in different online shops. Currently, many of the UK-specific sites only cater for a limited range of goods but, in line with the US equivalents, they should increase their range over the next year.

Bottom Dollar **www.bottomdollar.com**
Brilliant US-based site that lets you compare prices on a great range of products (not just the usual books and CDs). It's as fast and powerful as MySimon but its design is less jolly.

Buy.co.uk **www.buy.co.uk**
Find the cheapest electricity, gas or other utility – plus a good directory of shops on the web.

BuyBuddy **www.buybuddy.com**
Scour the web for the cheapest place to buy books, computers or home goods.

ComputerPrices **www.computerprices.co.uk**
Helps you find the cheapest computer kit in the UK. Compare these with US prices at BuyBuddy (**www.buybuddy.com**).

Even Better **www.evenbetter.com**

Helps find the cheapest book, video or CD on the market; covers a mix of both US and UK shops.

Internet Shopper **www.internetshopper.com**

Fast searching and neat results, lets you hunt through a reasonable range of products including books, music, video and software available at US stores. Without the range, polish or finish of MySimon or Bottom Dollar.

MySimon **www.mysimon.com**

One of the best from the US. At your command, dedicated bargain-hunter Simon runs off to scour the shelves of over 1,200 shops and then reports back. Covers every type of product, from computers to caviar – but you'll then need to check each result to see if they will ship overseas.

Price Offers **www.priceoffers.co.uk**

Buy one, get one free: this site has a different spin; it displays the current special offers and discounts from the major (real) supermarkets.

PriceScan **www.pricescan.com**

One of the few sites that will also compare delivery costs (for books) so that you get the truest price comparison. However, it can be slow and fiddly to use.

RoboShopper **www.roboshopper.com**

Displays the original vendor's page rather than a summary list, so it's much harder to compare prices. US based and not as quick nor as useful as MySimon or Bottom Dollar.

Shopgenie **www.shopgenie.com**

Fast, easy-to-use site that compares prices from the biggest online shops to find the cheapest books, videos, and CDs.

ShopSmart **www.shopsmart.co.uk**
The bargain finder's guide to the UK – fast, well designed and easy to use; great for comparing prices of over 90 stores selling books, videos, games and music.

Taxi **www.mytaxi.co.uk**
Impressive shopping tool to help find the cheapest book, video or CD – plus a good directory of shops.

Yahoo! **www.shop.yahoo.com**
Lets you search for goods from people who have set up their own Yahoo! store or the major stores on the web. The site's geared to the US consumer and it's not yet available on country-specific Yahoo! sites.

//SEARCHING FOR SHOPS

Finding shops on the net is not quite as easy as you might imagine. If you use a general-purpose search engine like Yahoo! or AltaVista and type in 'cotton shirts', you'll find hundreds of thousands of sites – some are shops, some are not. Instead, try using one of the specialist shop directories – each specializing in a different type or style of shop. For example, if you want to find the shops with the lowest prices, use a price-comparison search engine (see page 59). If you want to find a shop that's been approved and rated by other online consumers, try a directory like BizRate (**www. bizrate.com**). But half the fun of shopping on the net is to find new, specialist or obscure shops – and for these you will have to turn to a general search engine like AltaVista or Excite! Here's how to make sure you search efficiently.

Directories

As you browse the web, you'll soon find that there are hundreds of directories of shopping sites. Some of the biggest directories are provided by the major portal sites (that's Yahoo! Excite! Lycos and MSN), but these are not necessarily the best. You might find the range of shops, especially for non-US shoppers, is better on specialist directories.

The first question to ask is 'how did the directory choose the shop?' We picked the shops for our directory (in the second half of this book) by visiting each, seeing how they worked, if they shipped to an international address and provided a secure shopping environment. Some other directories are not so thorough. Many of the larger sites have commercial links with the shops that they list. For example, Yahoo! lists the shops that use its own shopping software system. And with others it's hard to know if the shop has got in through merit or advertising spend.

However, some of the best directories are independent. For the UK, start with ShopSmart, Buy.co.uk or EnterpriseCity or look at the Internet magazines that have directories of shops they have reviewed (for example Net magazine at **www.netmag.co.uk** and Zdnet at **www.zdnet.co.uk**). As an alternative, try Buyer's Index (**www.buyersindex.com**) with over 13,000 online (and mostly American) shops listed or About.com (**www.about.com**) that includes a vast directory of (mainly US) sites that the section editor has visited. And for a fellow consumer's view of what's available, have a look at BizRate (**www.bizrate.com**). Each of these directories reviews sites in a different way, and gives an individual view of the features and service available on the site.

Top directories of UK shops	
British Shopping	**www.british-shopping.com**
Buy.co.uk	**www.buy.co.uk**
iShop	**www.ishop.co.uk**
Lycos	**www.lycos.co.uk**

Shopping UK	**www.shoppinguk.co.uk**
ShopSmart	**www.shopsmart.com**
Shopping City	**www.shoppingcity.co.uk**
Taxi	**www.mytaxi.co.uk**
Top of the Shops	**www.topoftheshops.co.uk**

Top directories of US/international shops

About.com	**www.about.com**
BizRate	**www.bizrate.com**
Buyer's Index	**www.buyersindex.com**
Deal Pilot	**www.dealpilot.com**
Excite!	**www.excite.com/shopping/**
Lycos	**www.lycos.com**
MySimon	**www.mysimon.com**
Shops on the Net	**www.sotn.com**

//SEARCH ENGINES

Shopping directories are fine, but they generally contain just the most popular shops and so might miss out a listing for shops selling esoteric items such as Persian rugs (we don't: check the antiques section of the directory for Samarkand – **www.samarkand.co.uk**). The best way to hunt out your specialist site is to use your favourite general-purpose search engine, such as Excite! or Lycos. We prefer to save time by using the wonderful metasearch tools – these send your question to a dozen or so search engines and filter the answers for you.

General-purpose search engines

Search engines provide a vast index of almost every site on the Internet. Try them if you want to find something obscure, but you'll probably have to spend time wading through hundreds of results. Directories list fewer sites than an index – and the sites are normally checked for relevance and quality. Here are the major general-purpose search engines:

About	**www.about.com**
AltaVista	**www.altavista.com**
AskJeeves	**www.askjeeves.com**
FAST Search	**www.alltheweb.com**
Google	**www.google.com**
HotBot	**www.hotbot.com**
LookSmart	**www.looksmart.com**
WebCrawler	**www.webcrawler.com**

UK-specific search engines

Excite!	**www.excite.co.uk**
GOD	**www.god.co.uk**
Infoseek	**www.infoseek.co.uk**
Lycos	**www.lycos.co.uk**
UKPlus	**www.ukplus.com**
Yahoo!	**www.yahoo.co.uk**
Yell	**www.yell.co.uk**

Metasearching

The best way to search the web is to use a metasearch tool. Don't bother hiking from one general-purpose search engine to another, let the metasearcher do the legwork for you. Just type in your question and the metasearch site will automatically submit the question to all the main search engines and directories then filter the answers for relevance and present you with a manageable list of answers.

Sites like DogPile, All-in-One and Metacrawler are great for research to find the perfect shopping site. You get the benefit of all the search engines without the bother of visiting each one.

Top metasearch sites	
All-in-One	**www.allonesearch.com**
MetaCrawler	**www.metacrawler.com**
DogPile	**www.dogpile.com**
Savvy Search	**www.savvysearch.com**

Power searching

Whatever kind of search you do, if you're looking for a shop, you don't want thousands of hobby or enthusiast sites cluttering up the search results. A simple search for 'books' will display millions of hits to bookshops, libraries, research centres, author fan clubs, publishers and reading groups. You'll need to start using the 'power' search features that are part of all search engines and will help you refine your search.

To see how to improve your search technique, zip over to the friendliest search engine, HotBot (**www.hotbot.com**). You can quickly and easily define a complex search expression by choosing words that must or must not be matched. Simply click on the pull-down menus to create your search expression: it's really very easy to specify a complicated search that finds shops selling discount paperback science-fiction novels but not sites about authors of science-fiction novels.

If HotBot is not your usual search engine, you will have to use a rather less friendly notation system to refine your queries. Almost all the search engines (including Yahoo! and Excite!) let you refine your query using '+' and '-' symbols. If you put a '+' sign in front of a word, it means the word must be matched. And the '-' works in just the opposite way. So our previous query would be entered as 'bookshop +discount +science fiction +novel -hardback -author'.

The second way to power search is to use Boolean operators. These are the simple words AND, OR and NOT that you can insert between search terms. For example, if you want to find a site that sells imported bottled beers, you could enter the search term 'beer AND bottle AND imported'.

As you sift through your results, you'll soon realise that the engine is searching for all your words in any order. The next step to power status is to match an exact expression. To do this, enclose the expression in quote marks. For example, if you want to find a dairy that sells original Devon cream, type in 'Devon cream'. If you don't, you'll probably see sites that list the cream of Devon fishing and restaurants in Leeds offering Devon plaice with cream of mushroom sauce, and maybe even stranger things.

Email alerts for shoppers
Instead of spending hours hunting through auctions and classified ads trying to find a particular item, why not sit back and let the sites tell you when your item is up for sale? This feature, called an email alert, is fast becoming a standard on most of the better, larger classified ad and auction sites. It's simple: type in the name of the item you are hunting for and your email address and you'll get an email when it comes in.

Human intervention While a search engine tries to index everything that's available, directories (like Yahoo!) only include select sites in their directories. These are normally all picked by real people who visit the site, check that it's working and useful, then add it in the hallowed directory.

Some directories, such as LookSmart (**www.looksmart.com**) and About (**www.about.com**), go one step further – their editors write mini reviews of the site. This is great for surfers that prefer to trust the word of a fellow human, but it does limit the range of sites stored in the directory.

Specialist search software Instead of using a search engine on the Internet, you could use a special software package that runs on your PC. There are several specialist search tools on the market – they all cost good money and all effectively do the same as a metasearcher. Load the software on to your computer (it normally appears as a new button on your web browser toolbar) and type in your query – as complicated as you like. The software zips around the Internet to all the search engines to find sites that match your answer.

The more sophisticated versions will even answer questions from their own database. Many of these tools are now converting into web-based search sites, but there are still a few separate programs that work with your browser. Three of the better known are: CyberPilot (**www.netcarta.com**), Poke (**www.webprowler.com**) and the elderly WebCompass (**www.symantec.com**).

Finding similar sites A quick, neat and free way of adding a little zing to your web searches is to use a built-in feature of the new Microsoft Internet Explorer v5 and Netscape Navigator. When you've found a site you like, in Navigator, click on the 'What's Related' button and you'll see a menu of similar sites; in Internet Explorer, click on the 'Show Related Sites' menu: the screen splits and you'll see a list of sites covering the same subject. Unfortunately, it relies on a central database that knows how to link different sites and it only works some of the time.

The technology behind this neat trick is called Alexa. You can download a more powerful version of the same software that works with any browser. It installs itself as a tiny icon on the status bar at the bottom of the browser window. Download a free copy from **www.alexa.com**.

A new system called Real Names is being promoted as the alternative to all those confusing web addresses. Instead of typing in a company's address in your browser, just type in their company name. For example, to find the London Evening Standard newspaper site, either type in **www.thisislondon.co.uk** or just type their Real Name 'Evening Standard'. The system is part of Microsoft IE 5, or download free software from **www.realnames.com** for other browsers.

Dead addresses

Websites get launched, change name and get redesigned all the time. This makes it rather tricky for the search engines to keep track of what's going on. You'll see the problem when you start to search – many of the links thrown up just won't work when you click on them. Your browser will display a warning page that tells you the address cannot be found.

However, with some ingenuity and lateral thinking, you can still track down the site. One of the most common problems is that the site's designer changes the names of the individual pages within the site. This matters to the search engine but not to the site.

For example, if the search engine displays an entry as '**www.workingsite.com/buyThis/shops.html**' that doesn't work, you can try editing the address yourself to delete chunks from the address after each '/' symbol. Click on the address field at the top of your browser and use the arrow and delete keys to edit the address to read '**www.workingsite.com/buyThis/**'. Press Return to see if this works. You are now looking for a section of the site rather than a specific page.

4//SECURITY AND PAYMENT

When shopping on the Internet started, there were a lot of concerns about security. Was it safe to give people your credit card details over the Internet? What happened if your goods didn't turn up? Efficient security technology, called SSL (Secure Sockets Layer), was soon developed to provide a secure channel to let you enter your card details safely. Originally, many shops did not want to use this security feature because it was expensive and complicated to implement. Now, it's very cheap and easy to implement and any shop worth visiting should provide this feature for your protection.

As security has improved, so have the systems to speed payments. The most common currency on the web is still plastic and most of the bigger shops can authorise and debit your credit cards within seconds. There are new schemes being finalised that let you set up a kind of electronic wallet that you can use at any shop – getting over the bother of typing in your credit card details.

Just because the Internet is now secure enough to enter your credit card details does not mean it's without its problems. There are plenty of scams and frauds around, but follow the advice in the next few pages to see how to tell if a trader's legitimate and how to spot and avoid a scam. If you do have a problem, move on to the next chapter to read your consumer rights and how to complain and take action. So long as you follow a few basic guidelines, it is perfectly safe to shop online. In fact, so far there have been very few incidents of fraud and almost no thefts. Even the credit card issuing companies, VISA and MasterCard, both say it's safe and most credit cards, such as Egg and American Express, currently guarantee any online purchases made with its card.

//HOW CAN I TELL IF IT'S SAFE?

There are three things to look out for if you're interested in buying something online.

1 Authentication – are you absolutely sure that the company is what it claims to be?

2 Security – does the site provide a secure channel to allow you to enter personal credit card details?

3 Reputation – does the company have a good track record or is its customer service lousy?

Authentication You can be pretty certain that any high-street shop claiming to be, say, The Body Shop, actually is. But when you're online, how can you be sure that the site is really owned and operated by the people who claim to be doing so?

Any reputable website will include real-world contact details – such as address, phone number and contact for customer complaints. If you are suspicious, try the phone number to make sure it really works.

You can reassure yourself if you want by looking at one of the consumer-driven sites that rate online shops. Try the National Fraud Information Center (**www.fraud.org**) that lists bogus operators, or use our favourite, BizRate (**www.bizrate.com**), which lets consumers review and write comments about online shops. Or visit Which? (**www.which.net**) for a directory of the shopping sites that this consumer group recommends.

Remember, any reputable online shop will include a page that describes their security system and trading methods.

Security The Internet was not designed to transfer private, personal information: if you send anything over the Internet, it is transferred in a plain, readable form. It can easily be intercepted and read by hackers, should they choose to do so.

To counter this threat, Internet sites use technology to make sure that any important information is sent in an encrypted – scrambled – form. They do this by using secure websites that provide a safe channel of communication between your browser and the website. (Most shops use the SSL system but there are rivals, notably S-HTTP and SET.)

When you visit a secure website, the web server sends a signal to your web browser to ask it to switch to secure mode. When the browser replies, the server sends over its unique certificate of authentication (this is a unique series of numbers); the certificate is used by both browser and server as a key to create a special code that will scramble data as it's sent from one to the other. Anything you type in at the website is scrambled before it's transferred over the Internet – creating a secure channel. A determined hacker can still intercept the information you are sending to the website but, since it's encrypted, he or she can't read it.

Certificates of authentication

When a shop wants to set up a secure site, the company has to apply for a certificate of authentication. To get this document (that's actually an electronic file) it needs to provide adequate proof to an independent central authority that it is what (and who) it claims to be. The two biggest suppliers of certificates are VeriSign (**www.verisign.com**) and Thawte (**www.thawte.com**). Some sites will display their certificate or the VeriSign logo as proof of their status.To be sure, double-click on the closed padlock icon at the bottom of your browser window.

When the server and your browser have established the secure channel, a tiny closed padlock icon is displayed in the status bar at the bottom of the browser window. All the latest, current versions of web browsers support SSL. If you have an older version of a browser or just want to check everything is working, visit the VeriSign site (**www.verisign.com**) and use the online test that tells you if your browser is SSL-compatible.

SET – the next standard

There's a new secure way of sending credit card information over the Internet called SET (Secure Electronic Transmission) that will replace the existing SSL standard within the next year or two. SET is a combination of secure channel, electronic bank account and credit agency. It was developed by VISA and MasterCard as a better way to transfer payment details. As a consumer, you don't need to worry about SSL or SET – both are secure ways of ensuring that your personal information remains personal.

Smaller shops that don't have the money to invest in setting up a sophisticated secure shopping site can still sell their products on the web. Instead of using a secure site, you are asked to send your credit card details in an encrypted email message. The most popular – and secure – system for encrypting email messages is called PGP (pretty good privacy).

It's very easy to place a PGP order, but it's a little clumsier than using a slick shopping cart. If you haven't already got one, you'll need to install a PGP add-on to your email program (try the PGP home page at **www.pgp.com** for add-on software). The shop gives you a special code to enter when you send the message, so that only they can unscramble your email message. Very effective, but it's old-fashioned and too much extra effort for most shoppers.

Reputation It's hard to decide if a trader is reputable just by looking at their website so, if you have any doubts, you can check out the company by visiting one of the consumer monitoring or feedback sites. If there's a rogue trader on the web or even a big name that's not sorted out its web shop, you'll read about it at sites like the National Fraud Information Center (**www.fraud.org**), the Public Eye (**www.thepubliceye.com**) or even from consumer reviews at BizRate (**www.bizrate.com**).

As a final check, it might be worth visiting the consumer sites set up by the government, consumer organisations or trade organisations. For example, the Advertising Standards Authority (**www.asa.org.uk**) lists previous adjudications against fraudulent UK advertisers. In the US, try the Federal Trade Commission site (**www.ftc.gov**) for help and resources on scams, fraud and consumer rights and the Which? consumer site (**www.which.net**)

Top tips for safe shopping

1. Only shop at sites that give their contact details: address and phone number.
2. Ensure that the shop has a secure server set-up – indicated by the SSL standard. The site should promote this and explain it in its help page.
3. If possible, view the site's certificate of authentication supplied to sites using SSL. However, this is not always displayed.
4. Read the privacy policy and ensure that the site won't resell your personal details to a mailing list.
5. Ensure that there's a returns policy or guarantee available – it should be displayed in the help pages.

6 If you are suspicious, check if the company has a fraud listing or rates poorly with other consumers.

7 Pay by credit card to ensure that you have recourse to the card company. If you pay at an auction, try not to send cash or money transfer.

8 Make sure that there's a warranty and that this works in your country.

9 Ensure that you can see all the costs for your purchase – including shipping and taxes.

10 When you start, don't be too adventurous. It's best to try out shopping with names you know and trust.

//HOW SHOULD I PAY?

The most popular, convenient and safe way of paying for your shopping on the net is to use a credit card. However, there are dozens of different ways to handle and spend your money – some new schemes, some old. It's unlikely that you'll encounter these on your travels over the next few months, but it's still useful to familiarise yourself with alternative payment methods. You can find out what the professionals think of the different payment systems at **www.commerce.com**.

Here's a guide to the current ways of paying on the net.

Credit cards Use your standard, everyday credit card to pay for goods, giving the number, expiry date and your name to a secure website.

Pros: supported by almost every shop online. Easy, convenient and you have recourse to the card company if there are any problems.

Cons: a few credit card companies will charge you extra for sales on the Internet or will charge for international sales.

Links: www.visa.com; www.mastercard.com.

eCharge You pay for goods by charging the amount to your telephone bill. At the moment, UK company NetBanx (www.netbanx.co.uk) provides a similar service.

Pros: great if you don't have a credit card; you don't give out personal information.

Cons: there is a small extra charge.

Links: www.netbanx.com; www.echarge.com.

Digital cash Credit cards are too expensive and clumsy to make small purchases, such as the tiny charges levied by some websites to listen to music or read a book. Digital cash gets around this problem. You register with the digital cash provider and effectively set up an electronic 'wallet' that contains all your bank details. In return, you are issued with a unique security code that you can type in whenever you want to buy something at a participating shop. The shop charges your purchase to your wallet. The system ensures that you don't have to enter cumbersome and sensitive credit card details when shopping. Great idea, but none are in widespread use. However, the systems are getting established, the main ones being DigiCash (**www.digicash.com**) and InstaBuy (**www.instabuy.com**). Microsoft is also developing a formidable e-payment system (that's already part of your IE browser: look in the View/Tools section). The company is hoping to provide an 'electronic wallet' that stores details of all your credit cards and electronic cash. When you visit a shop, open your e-wallet and pay with card or cash.

Pros: easy to use and you don't have to give out your personal details each time you shop.

Cons: limited range of shops that accept digital cash and electronic wallets.

Links: www.instabuy.com; www.digicash.com; www.microsoft.com

Privacy safeguards

It's perfectly possible to browse at shopping sites without giving away any personal information. However, to take advantage of advanced features or create your own selection of your favourite subjects, you'll need to register. To register at almost any shopping site you'll need to type in your name and email address (and perhaps choose a password).

If you buy something, you'll certainly be asked for your name, address and phone number together with your email address and credit card details.

Before you hand over any personal information, make quite sure that the site has a privacy policy in place (it's normally in the 'help' or 'customer policy' pages). The site should state that your personal information will not be sold on to anyone else or used to send you unsolicited email. Some sites will give you the option to receive email marketing about similar products – called opt-in mailings.

If a shopping site doesn't have a privacy policy, think twice about using their services. You might find your email in-tray overflowing with unwanted adverts.

5//CONSUMER RIGHTS

Buy a chipped glass or a faulty videotape from your local shop and you can storm back in and demand a replacement. You might be surprised to learn that on the Internet, you've just the same rights – and, if you know the law, you can be sure you'll never be stuck with a dud deal.

If you buy anything in the UK, whether from the high street or on the Internet, you are covered under English or Scottish consumer law. If something doesn't work or it's not as described on the website or if the price is not as advertised, you can legally submit a claim against the company.

Basic rights British consumers have the right to insist that their goods are:

- Of satisfactory quality – they meet what is regarded as an acceptable standard of appearance and finish.
- Fit for their purpose – they must do what is detailed by the sales description. (If you ask for a Macintosh version of Quake and receive a PC version, it's not fit.)
- As described on the box or on the website. If you order a bookshelf described as solid mahogany but when it arrives you discover it's mahogany veneer, then it's not as described.

These points also cover goods bought in sales or on special offer. And if the goods are advertised as 'new', they must be unused.

An important point about statutory rights is that you must not wait too long to complain. You are allowed a reasonable time to try out the item before you are said to have 'accepted' the goods. If you wait too long, you will be said to have legally accepted the goods.

Goodwill and returns policies Most shops have extra policies in addition to your statutory rights. These are normally called goodwill policies, returns policies or sets of trading standards. The better online sites will include a page describing any extra rights you have as the consumer.

A good example is with clothing. If you buy your girlfriend what you think is a rather cool pale-blue leather trouser suit and you both hate it, your statutory rights won't help. However, the shop might be nice enough to let you return goods that you don't like.

Since the right to return goods that are not faulty is up to the shop, it is very important that you check their position on returns. If there's no mention of a returns policy on a website, telephone to ask.

Manufacturer guarantees In addition to your basic statutory rights and any extras provided by the shop, you should also get a manufacturer's guarantee. This provides an extra layer of protection but does not absolve the shop from its requirements. If the product doesn't work, go back to the shop first – even if they say it's 'the manufacturer's fault', they still have to comply with your statutory rights.

Watch this if you buy what's often called a 'grey' import – that is, an item imported from a different country. If you shop on the net, you are going to look at shopping sites in the UK, the US and around the world. If you buy simple, basic products such as books or music CDs, then there are few problems: it either works or it doesn't. You can't easily break it and you can return a cracked or snapped CD to the store for a refund.

The problems start when you try and buy complex goods – especially electronics and computers – over the net. The manufacturer's warranty of an item bought in the US does not normally extend to any other country. If you live in the UK and buy a laptop from the US (or any other country) you might save money, but the manufacturer's warranty won't be valid. If it goes wrong, you will have to pay to return it to the country or pay for local repairs. Before you buy any consumer electronics, make quite sure that you know the position regarding the manufacturer's warranty – check the manufacturer's site or call their local office.

Credit card insurance Most credit cards now cover goods purchased over the Internet for loss, damage or breakage at no extra charge. The insurance payout is likely to be for goods that cost between £100 and £30,000 – but check with the company that issues your card. American Express (though not technically a credit card) also insures you against fraud when you use AmEx to pay for goods online.

If the goods are never delivered or if the company goes bust before the item is delivered, you can claim against the card company (rather than the shop). Paying by credit card also makes it easier to trace payments or to dispute or stop a payment.

Your rights at auctions

Auctions are a hugely popular, enjoyable way of buying collectibles and junk on the Internet. The entire system, however, works on trust and provides you with very few consumer rights.

When you bid for an item, you enter a legal contract with the vendor and, for your part, you agree that you are happy with the condition of the item as seen. This means that it's very important to check the images of the item carefully and ask the vendor any questions before you bid.

If, when you receive the item, it's damaged or not the rare collectible you wanted then you could try and complain to the vendor. However, unless he or she is a dealer acting in a professional capacity, there's not much chance of a settlement. You can also complain to the auction site, but this won't get you very far since the site has no legal responsibility to either buyer or seller.

Since you have so few rights, you must make sure that you choose carefully before you bid. See Chapter 7 for full details on the safe way to play the auction game.

Almost all auction sites operate a rating system of sellers, for buyers – if you're unsure how trustworthy a seller is, read their reviews from previous customers. If you're unhappy with the service you received, say so in your review of this seller.

For a lot more about Internet auctions, see the **Virgin Internet Auction Guide**.

Complaints

If you have a grievance with an online trader and are getting nowhere, or simply cannot get through to the right person who will give you a straight answer, you can use an intermediary. Try one, or both, of these sites:

iLeveL **www.ilevel.com**
Helps sort out problems between shopper and shop.

Internet Consumer Assistance Bureau **www.isitsafe.com**
Acts as a middle ground between consumer complaints and merchant responses.

Returning goods

If you receive faulty goods, the company might try to make you return these at your own expense. Stand by your rights – you don't have to. If it's difficult or expensive to return, ask the company to come and collect it. However, if you are sending goods back under the shop's goodwill policy, you might well be asked to pay for the postage to return the product – often the case when exchanging clothes that are the wrong size.

If you want to return goods, telephone customer services immediately and send an email with details of your purchase. Make a note of the name of the person to whom you spoke and keep a copy of your email.

If you have received a faulty product and complained, you will probably be offered a range of options for refunds. The company might offer a replacement, free repair or a credit note against your next purchase. You don't have to accept any of these. You can insist on a full refund of the money you've paid. However, if you are returning goods under the shop's goodwill policy, they might instead offer you a credit note or voucher to spend on other goods in their shop.

//ADDRESS BOOK

Where to complain

If you didn't get satisfaction from the people who sold you the goods, you can start to complain to other people about the company. Here's a list of the best places to lodge a complaint:

Advertising Standards Association **www.asa.org.uk**
Complain about false advertising or claims.

Financial Services Association **www.fsa.gov.uk**
All sites offering some form of financial services are normally governed by the FSA. If you are unhappy, complain.

National Association of Citizens Advice Bureaux **www.nacab.org.uk**
Will help lodge a complaint and work with you to resolve a consumer dispute with a supplier within the UK or the EU.

Office of Fair Trading **www.oft.gov.uk**
Does not normally deal with consumer complaints but its site provides plenty of help for consumers and it will step in where there are recurrent problems.

Trading Standards **www.tradingstandards.gov.uk**
This government body has the power to investigate claims against false service or supply of goods and it's a good place to start when you've been scammed by an online shop.

Lists of the bad guys

Bad, Better and Best Businesses Bulletin Board **www.webBbox.com**
Database of who's good and bad news for shoppers on the net.

Better Business Bureau www.bbb.org
Help for businesses that want to be good, for consumers that want to complain and a directory of nice people to deal with.

BizRate www.bizrate.com
Brilliant database of reports and reviews written by consumers – get the low-down on the low-life.

Internet Advocacy Center www.consumeradvocacy.com
Good resource about fraud on the net.

National Fraud Information Center www.fraud.org
Hear about frauds as they happen – geared to reporting US fraudsters.

Public Eye www.thepubliceye.com/review.htm
Rating shop sites for consumers.

Web Assurance Bureau www.wabureau.com
Consumer agency that keeps archives of who's done what.

Safe-shopping programmes

Consumers' Association www.which.net
Provides a (short) list of online traders who comply with all the requirements on consumer protection.

MasterCard Shop Smart www.mastercard.com/shopsmart
Programme that promotes safe shopping (sites that use SSL secure servers).

Auction safety

iEscrow www.iescrow.com
A safe middle ground for shoppers that want to buy from auctions and classifieds on the web.

TradeSafe **www.tradesafe.com/tradesafe**
Safe middleman that helps you buy from auction or classified sites.

Privacy

TRUSTe Privacy Program **www.truste.org**
Sites that respect privacy of shoppers.

6//AUCTIONS

The thrill of the bid, getting top quality at rock-bottom prices, or simply the only way to get rid of your junk. Whatever the reason, online auctions are the most active and most popular way of shopping on the net at the moment. Online auctions, such as those offered by QXL, Ebid, eBay, Sotheby's or E-Swap, are definitely among the most active, fun and risky parts of the Internet shopping experience. Most of the auction sites are run as personal auctions – this means one individual puts an item up for sale and any other visitor can bid for it. There are also third-party auctions (where the auction site sells off items for another company) and traditional auctions, which are held in a normal auction house and you simply participate via the net.

Costs

If you want to buy at an auction, it should be free. You pay only your bid and any postage to deliver the item. If you want to sell an item at an online auction, most sites will charge you (although Up4Sale lets you sell for free). The standard practice is to charge a modest listing fee – generally under £1 – for including your item and a second percentage-based fee (normally 5% for items under £100 and 2.5% over this limit) once you've sold your item. You shouldn't be charged if the item does not sell or does not meet its reserve price. Check the fee structure carefully before you decide to sell – some sites' fees are so high they hardly make it worth selling your old junk.

Internet auctions have suffered a tarnished image as a hotbed of stolen goods and petty fraud. In fact, most vendors are selling perfectly good, legitimate items and auctions continue to be fantastically popular. However, you should be careful before you join in.

Registration Before you can start bidding for an item advertised in an auction, you will need to register with the site. This normally means providing your home address, phone number and other personal details. Some auction sites (such as QXL) also ask for your credit card details to ensure that you will pay when you've bought something.

Once you have registered, you can start bidding for items. In most online auctions, the item is available for bids for a limited period of just a few days. If, at the end of this period, yours is the highest bid then you win the auction and the item is yours.

Making bids When you bid at an auction, you immediately acknowledge that you have read and agreed to the auction site's conditions. Because of this, you should read the conditions – they vary from site to site. Most will carefully explain that when you bid you are entering a legal contract with the seller of the item. If you have a winning bid, you legally must pay the seller, even if you have now changed your mind.

There is no point going back to the auction site itself as it has no legal responsibility in the process and is simply an 'enabling' technology to bring together buyers and sellers. The bottom line is, if there's a problem then you'll have to try to sort it out with the seller.

Playing it safe To avoid the bother of risking your money on an item you've only seen as a grainy image on screen, some auction sites now provide extra safety features to help prevent problems. For example, Ebid has a delayed payment system: the buyer deposits the money in a safe account with Ebid and this is only released to the seller when the buyer acknowledges receipt of the item.

Third-party specialist companies work in a similar way as middlemen for other online auctions. The popular PayPal (**www.paypal.com**), i-Escrow (**www. iescrow.com**) and Tradesafe (**www.tradesafe.com**) all try and help the seller get their money and provide a guarantee for the buyer. However, most sellers don't like either system and will generally not accept bids if final payment is via these routes. And, as a buyer, there's nothing you can do about this except wait for another, more co-operative seller to enter the ring.

Dealers place many auction items and, if they are operating in a professional way, they will extend standard dealer terms to you as a buyer. Many items will include either a returns clause or a modest guarantee of authenticity from the dealer. Some even go so far as to provide proof of previous ownership (often called 'provenance'). The bigger dealers will let you pay by credit card and will supply masses of photographs and extra information about the goods, and answer any questions promptly.

Complaints and feedback

Most auction sites don't want bad publicity, but equally they don't want to get involved between buyers and sellers. To help out, almost all the auction sites provide user feedback or rating systems. Any registered user can rate a seller and attach a comment about their products or conduct. If you are unhappy with a purchase, the best place to complain is by rating the seller poorly and explaining your complaint – it will help to deter other buyers from dealing with this person again. If the vendor is a trustworthy dealer, you should see a whole list of happy customer reports. If the person or company is selling for the first time, there'll be no reports. And if the seller has changed identity by reregistering, this should be displayed to warn you to ask why.

Online auctions can be dangerous places because there's so little in the buyer's favour. You get the opportunity of a low price but, unless you tread carefully, you could end up with a dud.

Here are our essential tips to help you safeguard your rights:

- Read the auction's policy of sales before you register. Some might provide warranties, guarantees or a delayed payment system – but most won't.
- Most auction sites operate a rating system that allows buyers to comment on a seller – read the comments, but remember that they might not all be genuine.
- When you see an item you want to bid for, take your time to find out as much as you can about the item. If there's not enough displayed, email the seller and ask. If you're not happy with the answers, steer clear of this item.
- The safest route is to only bid at an auction site that includes guarantees, such as Sotheby's (**www.sothebys.com**), or bid and pay using i-Escrow or Tradesafe. Unfortunately, many sellers won't accept this. The second-best route is to pay by credit card. Never agree to pay by cash or bank draft.
- If you win the auction, get in touch with the seller and arrange for shipping via insured courier or registered mail (you'll have to pay). If the seller claims the item must have been damaged in transit, claim from the courier company.
- If, when you receive the item, it is damaged or not as described, get in touch with the seller immediately. Ask nicely to return the item or have it repaired at the seller's cost. It's unlikely to work, but it's worth a try.
- If you cannot agree with the seller, approach the auction site with the complaint and post a message about the problem to deter other buyers.

//ADDRESS BOOK

Starting points

Auction Guide **www.auctionguide.com**

Going, going, go to this guide to online auctions around the world. For a similar idea, but with a different approach, try the Auction Channel (**www.theauctionchannel.co.uk**), which combines traditional auction house sales into one site.

Auction Connect **http://auctionconnect.lycos.com**

Handy service from Lycos – lets you search for items up for sale in a couple of dozen auctions from eBay to Amazon. It'll even send you an email or ICQ message when an auction item is about to close.

AuctionWatch **www.auctionwatch.com**

Fantastically useful site that searches dozens of the main auction sites to help you find the item you're after.

BldFind **www.vsn.net**

Search engine that hunts through a couple of dozen online auctions but doesn't always find much.

iCollector **www.icollector.com**

Bid for items from auction houses from around the world – best of all, research through past auction catalogues for information and price guides. A must-see site for any collector.

Internet Auction List **www.internetauctionlist.com**

The largest and most comprehensive list of auctions on the net.

Online auctions

Auction Universe **www.auctionuniverse.com**

Online auctions with some great features, but without the buzz and traffic of QXL or eBay. Best feature: there's a guarantee that takes the risk of fraud out of buying at the auction.

Bid-4-It **www.bid4it.com**

Bid for business or consumer goods – the difference is that you set the price you're prepared to pay and wait for a seller to match it. Seems best for industrial equipment and guns.

bluecycle.com **www.bluecycle.com**

Rather quiet new auction site - which is a shame, since it's easy to use and even donates a chunk of its profits to charity.

Bonhams **www.bonhams.com**

One of the few traditional auction houses that allows you to bid online; subscribe (for free) and you'll get all the details for the auction.

Christies **www.christies.com**

Renowned in the traditional, real-world auction circuit, but still experimenting with a low-key website.

For a lot more about Internet auctions, take a look at the Virgin Internet Auction Guide.

---

eBay **www.ebay.com**

Monster US auction site; hundreds of thousands of items for sale, bid from around the world – but check with the vendor on shipping costs. The UK version (**www.ebay.co.uk**) is a nice idea, but has only a fraction of the number of items for sale.

Ebid **www.ebid.co.uk**

Great looking site but not as much going on as at QXL.

E-swap **www.eswap.co.uk**

Not a swap-shop as you might imagine, but a rather neat person-to-person auction site, specialising in computers and music gear.

Global Auction Online **http://global-auction.com**

Free auction – in that there are no charges for sellers – but a very poor selection up for grabs.

Humpty Dumpty **www.humpty.com**
Basic, friendly auction that's still rather quiet.

Popula **www.popula.com**
Specialises in vintage and collectible items like books, music and Hollywood ephemera. These are person-to-person auctions and a good place to pick up unusual collectibles. Easy to use and friendly.

Pottery Auction **www.potteryauction.com**
Splendidly obsessive person-to-person site selling all types of pottery from cookie jars to classic vases.

QXL **www.qxl.co.uk/**
Buy or sell goodies at the top UK auction site. Unlike the other auction sites, QXL sells gear itself, as well as allowing anyone to sell their belongings in personal auctions.

Shop4u.com **www.shop4u.com**
An oddball auction in which you can either post an entry with the details of an item and the price you want to pay for it or you can act as a shopper and post a price at which you've seen the item. If you're a shopper and supply the lowest price for a buyer, you'll get $5 for your efforts.

Sotheby's **www.sothebys.com**
Impressive, packed auction site from the established brand; easy to use, masses of antiques and paintings and guarantees for buyers.

Up4Sale **http://up4sale.com**
Sell anything here for free. Owned by the massive eBay online auction site.

WhatAmIBid **www.whatamibid.com**
Looking for a missing beanie baby? Here's a good place for collectibles.

Auctions by companies

DealDeal.com **www.dealdeal.com**
Consumer electronics and household goods on sale as job lots at cut prices. New and reconditioned equipment with warranties, guarantees and plenty of information.

Egghead.com **www.surplusauction.com**
US computer supplier selling off mostly software, hardware and accessories – good place to buy just-past-it kit. Will ship to the UK but you need to phone through to confirm details.

First Auction **www.firstauction.com**
From the people that bring you Home Shopping Network on TV. Here, they parade goods past you in short, flash auctions lasting just 30 minutes.

OnSale **www.onsale.com**
Two ways of buying computers, sports, travel, holidays and even consumer electronics: either bid at the auction or go for the wholesale price, you decide which. Great prices, good backup and shipping around the world – but the warranties are unlikely to follow the computers outside North America.

Sporting Auction **www.sportingauction.com**
One company's auction of brand name sports kit, equipment and accessories. Almost all with guarantees – you'll have to pay extra to ship out of the US.

TravelBids Travel Discount Auction **www.TravelBids.com**
You say where you want to go and a whole bunch of hungry travel agents bid for your custom. Unfortunately, you'll need a friend who lives in the US to order the tickets.

Winebid.com **www.winebid.com**
Impressive range of premium wines on offer in monthly sales.

7//SHOPPING DIRECTORY

Guide to the directory

This section covers 800 or so of the most interesting, useful and friendly shopping sites around. If you're looking for a particular product – like books, music or videos – try the appropriate section or browse through a general department store or mall.

We chose these shopping sites after visiting and browsing through their range of products. No, we didn't spend our money at each – but we did go through all the steps required to place an order. We also checked that the shopping system was secure and, importantly, that the shop would serve international customers. All the shops here are secure except for a few of the smallest niche shops that don't yet have secure servers – and we've mentioned that in the write up.

As you browse around you'll find plenty of new sites. If you think it's worth including in the next edition of this guide, we would be delighted to hear from you (email us at response@virgin-pub.co.uk). We didn't include companies that only published their catalogue and referred customers to their local shop – as a web-shopper, you deserve better than that!

Before you run amok through the directory waving your credit card, here's a quick overview of the thousands of sites vying for your custom. It's relatively easy to set up an online shop, so the range of shops is vast and the way you place your order and pay for the goods varies a lot from site to site. Most shops fall into one or other of the following categories:

Individual shops and distributors

The bulk of the shops listed in this book are individual companies that let you order and pay for products online. These might be tiny specialist suppliers like Billy Bob Teeth (**www.billybobteeth.com**) or global brands like Dell (**www.dell.co.uk**). However, the common factor across all these sites is that they only sell one range of products.

The shops all offer an electronic shopping basket to collect your goods as you browse or search the list of products in the catalogue. Once you have finished shopping at this site, click on the Checkout button and you are presented with the list of items in your basket, the bill and a form to fill in with your credit card and delivery details. When you click Pay, the software checks that your credit card is valid and displays a confirmation note. Many sites will also send you an email to confirm your order. Now, just sit and wait for the goods to arrive.

Shopping centres and malls

At the start of the net shopping revolution, the best way of setting up a shop was in a mall – a group of unrelated shops gathered together under one umbrella site, such as BarclaySquare (set up by Barclays Bank). It provides a set of guarantees for consumers and vendors and a single route to a good range of shops.

The shops in the mall use the same shopping basket idea as an individual store and you can normally take your basket from one shop to another in the mall. These malls can often provide far better consumer guarantees and policies than individual shops, but they can be claustrophobic, given the vast range of specialist shops on the web.

Auctions

The idea behind online auctions is a simple one: anyone can advertise an item, with a description and usually a photograph. Any other visitor can put in a bid for the item. Generally, the auction for the item stays open for a week or two (the seller determines this) and might or might not have a reserve price.

Anyone (who has registered by entering in his or her name and address at the site) can bid in any auction. Simply type in the price you want to bid, or a maximum bid, and click the Bid button. Your new bid is displayed as the current highest offer for the item – till someone else bids more. You can bid as many times as you like for the item till the time limit for the auction is reached. The person who has submitted the highest bid wins the auction. It's now up to the buyer and seller to exchange money and goods.

The entire system works on trust and it's up to the bidder to check that the item is what they want (either by checking the description carefully or emailing the seller).

Unlike the previous two types of site, you don't get to actually pay for the product online. Instead, you're bidding for an item and then have to arrange traditional payment (e.g. credit card or money transfer) by speaking with the seller or by paying via an online middleman company (such as i-Escrow or Tradesafe). See Chapter 6 for details on how to pay securely and minimise the risks when using online auctions.

Classified ads

Another alternative route to bargains and secondhand items is to look through the classified ads. You can't buy or pay for the item online – it's just an alternative way of advertising that's convenient for both buyer and seller.

There's no central directory of classified ads. Instead, these appear in listings magazines or as a feature of specialist sites. For example, the popular *Loot*, *Exchange and Mart* and *AutoTrader* listings magazines are all online. You'll have to contact the vendor to arrange viewing and eventual purchase.

There are even some newsgroups that carry classified ads: pop up your newsgroup reader and search for 'wanted' or 'classified' for a list of subject groups that let you post ads. And don't, whatever you do, post classified ads in any other newsgroup – you'll be flamed (sent tons of abusive email) if you do.

Coupons and affiliate schemes

If you have your own website, you can make money by referring visitors to another commercial site. This system, called affiliate marketing, is widespread – find out more at AffiliatesDirectory (**www.affiliatesdirectory.com**).

In faithful reflection of the real world, electronic coupons hit the net a couple of years ago (the best supplier is probably eSmarts at **www.esmarts.com**). Visit a coupon site, pick up an electronic coupon, take it to an online retailer and present it to save money.

Despite making the process very easy, most online shops won't take coupons (they're already down to the barest of margins) and the system simply doesn't work for international shoppers.

But don't give up. There are several schemes that were created just for the Internet (rather than modifying the idea of coupons for the net). Try Click Rewards (**www.clickrewards.com**) or the I-points scheme (**www.ipoints.co.uk**) that lets you rack up special points as you spend in participating shops – then trade in the points for free books, CDs or flights. Another is Beenz (**www.beenz.com**) that lets you collect points as you visit any of the affiliated sites. You don't have to spend anything, just visit the sites and click on the Beenz button. Once you've enough Beenz currency, you can trade them for discounts at affiliated sites. It's a clever – and free – marketing tool that's rapidly attracting new affiliates and users.

And don't forget to use your usual affinity card if you're shopping in Tesco, Sainsbury's or any other store – you can still rack up points for items bought online.

Top tips for safe shopping

1 Only enter your credit card and personal details on a secure site (that has the closed padlock icon in the bottom line of the browser).

2 If you're unsure, check the consumer review sites (see page 82).

3 Only shop with companies that provide a full contact address and phone number.

4 Try to stick to shops you know or can phone to check that they exist.

5 Ensure that delivery costs to your country are made clear before you order.

6 Keep a note of the transaction number.

7 Request delivery by recorded post or courier – for proof of delivery.

8 If a package is damaged, refuse to accept it and call the company.

9 Make sure that you have rights of return on faulty or damaged goods.

10 Ensure that if you're expecting new goods, you receive them rather than a used product.

Wondering where to go first? Try these sites for a flavour of what's out there:

1. Amazon (**www.amazon.co.uk**) – still just about the best bookshop that's busy, friendly and informative.
2. Blackstar (**www.blackstar.co.uk**) – the top choice for videos and DVDs.
3. Tesco (**www.tesco.co.uk**) – all your groceries delivered with style.
4. Landsend (**www.landsend.com**) – simple, cotton clothes in a clean and airy site.
5. Softwareparadise (**www.softwareparadise.com**) – all the software you'll ever need.
6. VirginWines (**www.virginwines.co.uk**) – easy way to buy a good range of wines.
7. Unbeatable (**www.unbeatable.co.uk**) – great prices on electrical goods.
8. Wallpaperstore (**www.wallpaperstore.com**) – more wallpaper styles than you could imagine.
9. Animail (**www.animail.co.uk**) – masses of goodies for your pets.
10. FAO Schwarz (**www.fao.com**) – fantastic range of thousands of toys for sale.

//ADDRESS BOOK

//ANTIQUES AND COLLECTIBLES

There's no need to spend Saturdays scrabbling around car boot sales or markets in the hope of finding a rare collectible; they're all on the net. Dealers have seized the opportunity to advertise to a worldwide audience of collectors, making this section one of the most active areas in the shopping landscape. Here's a great range of shops that specialise in antiques and collectibles – but don't forget that the auction sites (notably QXL, eBay and eSwap) see most of their activity in sales of collectibles. Find Hollywood autographs by the hundredweight, antique furniture in Wales or tin-plate toys from Japan – all neatly priced and ready to be shipped back to your home.

Starting point

---

iCollector **www.icollector.com**

A must-see site for any collector. Bid for items from auction houses from around the world – best of all, research through past auction catalogues for information and price guides.

Celebrity collectibles

Alfie's Autographs of Hollywood **www.alfies.com**

The price of fame – thousands of autographs from actors and celebs, old and new. This is where to get underwear signed by Aerosmith and more conventional things signed by Nirvana.

Autos and Autos **www.autosautos.com**

Autographs and documents from an eclectic mix of air and military figures (and actors who've played them). Letters from J Edgar Hoover, Henry Fonda's signature.

Popula **www.popula.com**
Person-to-person auction site that specialises in vintage and collectible books, music and Hollywood ephemera. It's a good place to pick up unusual collectibles – and is easy to use and friendly to new shoppers.

Recollections **www.recollections.co.uk**
Ticket stubs to T-shirts – rock memorabilia for collectors.

Roslyn Herman & Co. **www.roslynherman.com**
Cast-offs from the celebs – you could find John Wayne's lighter or Marlene Dietrich's compact. Everything is backed by letters of authenticity.

Someone Special **www.someonespecial.com**
Collectors collect here – thousands of items for sale.

Wonderful World of Animation **www.animationartgallery.com**
Original sketches and cells from classic animated films. And sceptics can get a letter of authenticity included.

Antiques

Architectural Heritage **www.architectural-heritage.co.uk**
Antique-panelled-rooms and iron garden furniture to add period style to your home.

Harman's Antiques **http://members.aol.com/antiquetoo/**
A friendly place to shop for a decent range of antique furniture – dining tables to chests. Again, order via phone – but the prices are listed together with descriptions and very good

Hingstons of Wilton Antiques **www.hingstons-antiques.freeserve.co.uk**
A good range of antique furniture (and even a few clocks) – nice layout, very good photos and lots of details but, annoyingly, you have to call for pricing.

Huntington Antiques **www.huntington-antiques.com**
Vast, carved medieval and gothic furniture items are the speciality – you can't order from the site, but the catalogue is up to date and you can phone through your order.

Medusa Ancient Art **http://anawati.com**
Astonishing range of ancient art and antiquities from Roman, Egyptian, Greek and other cultures. Beautiful stonework, bronze and jewellery. Not cheap and no online ordering, but at this price you can afford a call to the US office.

Samarkand Galleries **www.samarkand.co.uk**
Antique rugs and textiles from Persia and the Caucasus.

Worldwide Antiques **www.worldwide-antiques.com/home.htm**
Modest selection of nice antique furniture, prints and collectibles. Online ordering is just as ancient as the exhibits, but adequate.

Ephemera

Eureka, I Found It **www.eureka-i-found-it.com**
Finally, you know where to find that antique steam engine, vintage brass buttons or costume jewellery.

Pewter Collectibles **www.pewter.co.uk**
Tankards and flasks – in pewter – that are meant more for display than drinking.

//ART AND POSTERS

Match high-quality images, cheap gallery space and a global audience and you'll find the web is the perfect show-space for any piece of art. You'll find specialists selling modern art, prints of yachts, and lots and lots of posters. With any type of fine art, provenance (the previous owners and history) are important, so make sure that you get full details of authenticity before you pay – and ensure that adequate packing and return-rights are included.

Art Planet **www.artplanet.com**
Every fine art site listed to help you find museums (and their shops), artists, galleries and suppliers.

World Wide Arts Resources **http://wwar.com**
Want art? Here's a vast mass of links. Not as well organised as Art Planet, but a good place to start exploring.

Original art

African Marketplace **www.afrikunda.com**
The heat of the African plains shimmers through this site – selling authentic art from masks to paintings. You can order online, but you'll have to pay by money order to the US, which is a pain. Still, it's easier to arrange than a trip to the Big Country.

Art.Net **www.art.net**
A community for wandering artists and art lovers. Artists' studios and galleries show art forms from sculpture to poetry.

Art-Smart **www.art-smart.com**
Hundreds of artists and their portfolios posing for potential collectors.

Flowers East **www.flowerseast.co.uk**
Contemporary works by some of the best British artists housed in cool warehouse galleries in the east of London and the west coast of the US.

Posters and prints

Art **www.art.com**

One of the neatest, smartest shops on the net: start by choosing an image from the vast Hulton Getty image library of over 100,000 famous works, then choose a frame and see what it'll look like on-screen. Best of all, you can return the framed art if you hate it – but you'll have to pay the shipping back to Illinois.

art e-Store **http://art-estore.com/prfa/index.htm**

Fine art prints and posters, things to hang them on, art books to read, and plenty more.

Art Republic **www.artrepublic.com**

Several thousand posters of well-known works of art, together with books and an impressive guide to the current art scene.

Legends Concert Posters **www.concertposters.com**

Pin up Elvis – one of over 4,000 original concert, theatre and festival posters. Also does records and sheet music.

Dr. Z Cinema Posters **www.blarg.net/~dr_z/Main.html**

Psycho to *Breakfast at Tiffany's* – a wonderful range of classic vintage posters.

GB Posters **www.gbposters.co.uk**

More entertainment posters than you've got walls – classic music, film and TV. It's a UK company, so you could save on your shipping.

Lahaina Printsellers Ltd **www.printsellers.com**

Antique maps and prints to line your study – good-looking reproductions and originals for sale.

Online Posters **www.onlineposters.com**

Classy art posters of architectural elements and other stuff.

PosterWorld **www.posterworld.com**
Racy women for the garage wall. Lads only.

Postrczar **www.postrczar.com**
Fabulous range of original classic East European posters from the Communist years. Propaganda, theatre and art, shipped from the US – land of the free.

Red Lion Racing Team **http://visref.com/redlion**
Original classic automobile racing posters – the ordering system's antique, but the (mostly US) posters are wonderful.

Shorelines Gallery **www.shorelines.co.uk**
Sailing prints – yachts and blazers in action.

Artist supplies

The biggest names in the industry (such as Windsor and Newton) have wonderful sites, but they're just catalogues with nothing for sale. Luckily, enterprising art lovers have stepped in to ensure you can buy original Chinese brushes and inks, oils and canvas.

Arts Encaustic **www.encaustic.com**
Selling everything you'll need to make swirly patterns with melted wax.

art e-Store **http://art-estore.com/prfa/index.htm**
Under-construction site promising artists' materials, portfolios, picture hanging and lighting systems, wood display easels and much, much more.

Cass Arts **www.cass-arts.co.uk**
Everything you need to create your masterpiece – over 10,000 art products in store, plus tips, advice and step-by-step lessons to get you started.

Guanghwa Company Ltd, UK **www.guanghwa.co.uk**
Brushes, inks and paper to produce Chinese art and calligraphy.

Heaton Cooper **www.heatoncooper.co.uk**
Great range of paints, brushes and materials from this tiny shop in deepest Cumbria.

Heffers **www.heffers.co.uk**
Best known as a bookshop, it stocks a surprisingly wide range of artists' materials – brushes, paints and mounts.

Lawrence – Artists' Materials **www.lawrence.co.uk**
Old-established artist and printmaker's supplier – from ink rollers to acrylics.

Willow Fabrics **www.willowfabrics.com**
Material for embroidery – canvasses, yarns and silks, or ready-made kits; halfway towards online ordering with prices and a form to fax or email.

//BABIES AND TODDLERS

Hardworking, over-tired parents rarely have enough time to sit down, so the promise of quick, simple and cheap baby stuff and supplies is a big draw. The Internet has plenty of specialist shops that let you order clothes, nursery kit or even a regular supply of nappies. However, you'll find that the best range of food and milk is stocked by online supermarkets like Sainsbury's and Tesco (see 'Food', below). If you're looking for clothes, games or equipment for older children, try the relevant sections in this book – many of the shops stocking adult clothes also have a line in togs for the kids.

Babies Я Us **www.babiesrus.co.uk**
Everything to carry, clothe, feed and mop up after your new baby – from the Toys Я Us company.

Babycare Direct **www.babycare-direct.co.uk**
Kit to help care for your new baby. A simple design hides a mass of products with excellent pix and descriptions.

Baby Directory **www.babydirectory.com**
An essential bookmark for any parent – absolutely everything you need to know for where to go, where to buy and how to look after your offspring, from pregnancy to babies, toddlers and children under five. Okay, you can't actually buy anything, but it's too good to miss!

families.co.uk **www.families.co.uk**
Where to go and what to do on rainy days, sunny days or holidays. Now flip to 'Travel' to book it.

Baby Planet **www.bbplanet.dircon.co.uk**
Like, cool, babe – tie-dyed T-shirts and Y-fronts for 0–6-year-olds direct from trendy Notting Hill.

Babyworld **www.babyworld.co.uk**
Almost the whole baby world is here – products, features, health news and special offers for babies (and mums) – great design that's by far the nicest of the baby sites around.

Bearworld **www.bearworld.co.uk**
Bears in every shape and form. And over 50 versions of Po, Tinky Winky and gang (Tubby beanie bags, radios, talking models ... you get the idea).

Bumble Bugs **www.bumblebugs.co.uk**
Kit out the small folk (up to 4) with clothes, toys and nursery essentials.

Character Warehouse Ltd **www.character-warehouse.com**
Barney, Noddy, Bananas in Pyjamas, Rosie and Jim and the usual TV suspects available in games, puzzles, toys – even wallpaper – for mad-keen kids.

Nappies Direct **www.nappies-direct.co.uk**
Terry and flannel nappies direct from shop to bot.

Snugger Baby Wear and Bedding **www.btinternet.com/~weathervain/SNUGGER.html**

Sleeping bags for babies – not for camping but to help settle and for car trips. Try them.

Urchin **www.urchin.co.uk**

Funky furniture and accessories for kids.

//BANKING AND PERSONAL FINANCE

Make the most of your finances with help from the Internet. Save money on insurance, pick the perfect mortgage or trade shares online. Helping on the revolution is the trend of high-street banks to offer you the chance to manage your account online, via the Internet. Many of the major banks (like FirstDirect, Barclays and the Royal Bank of Scotland) let you shuffle money between accounts and pay your bills from your PC. But the majority of these online banks aren't accessible via the public Internet; instead, they have set up their own private networks, used in the same way as the Internet but very separate for obvious security reasons.

Make the most of your buying power with the online guides that help maximise savings and minimise bills. Blay's Guides sort through the savings accounts on offer and will show you where to find the best rates. If you're spending rather than saving, Car Quote and Screen Trade will help you cut your payments, while MoneyNet will send you the best deal from credit card companies.

Before you tackle the stock markets, use the clear, concise financial guides – the best are from FTQuicken and MoneyWorld – to understand how to understand the markets and make the most of your money. Once you're online, you'll find that you have access to the same instant, real-time share price information as the professionals and can deal online and manage your portfolio cheaply and efficiently.

Banks online

Abbey National	**www.abbeynational.co.uk**
Alliance and Leicester	**www.allianceandleicester.co.uk**
Barclays	**www.barclays.co.uk**
Co-op	**www.co-operativebank.co.uk**
Egg	**www.egg.com**
First direct	**www.firstdirect.co.uk**
Halifax	**www.halifax.co.uk**
HSBC (Midland)	**www.banking.hsbc.co.uk**
LloydsTSB	**www.lloydstsb.co.uk**
Nationwide	**www.nationwide.co.uk**
Natwest	**www.natwest.co.uk**
Royal Bank of Scotland	**www.royalbankscot.co.uk**

Credit cards

If your credit card isn't listed here, ask the company that provides it about its plans for the Internet.

MasterCard	**www.mastercard.com**
VISA	**www.visa.com**
American Express	**www.amex.com**
Barclaycard	**www.barclaycard.co.uk**
Charity Credit Card	**www.charitycard.co.uk**

Save as you spend – apply online for a card that gives money to charities (such as Battersea Dogs Home) as you use your credit card.

Credit Card Advice **www.moneyextra.co.uk/products/credit_cards.asp**

Clever database lets you compare the rates and deals from over 80 providers to choose the best for your spending patterns.

Footballcard Mastercard **www.footballcard.co.uk**
Get a credit card supporting your fave team.

Shares

Charles Schwab **www.schwab-worldwide.com**
Buy, sell or research from the biggest online broker. Excellent resources, graphing and investment advice, but you'll need to register and deposit money first.

E*Trade **www.etrade.co.uk**
The new pretender to Schwab's crown as top online broker. A slick and info-rich site that helps you research, manage and trade shares. Low-cost trades, but you'll have to pay a modest monthly fee for research.

Stocktrade **www.stocktrade.co.uk**
Simple, straightforward execution-only online trading.

Financial advice

Blay's Guides **www.blays.co.uk**
Which savings account provides the best interest rates.

Financial Information Net Directory **www.find.co.uk**
As the title says, it's full of information about anything financial – from pensions to ISAs.

FT Quicken – Personal Finance **www.ftquicken.co.uk**
Good advice for the average financial consumer. Keep your money healthy and stay up to date with news and info on money products.

MoneyExtra **www.moneyextra.com**
Compare mortgages, credit cards, savings accounts, pensions, life assurance – then pick the best.

Moneynet **www.moneynet.co.uk**
Choose the perfect credit card or mortgage. Fill in a form and you'll be sent details of dozens of deals.

MoneyWeb **www.moneyweb.co.uk**
Good, free information on how and where to invest.

Money World **www.moneyworld.co.uk**
An impressively complete site that tries – and generally succeeds – to cover all aspects of personal finance. You can check share prices, currency movements, view mortgage rates, tax bands and use their online calculators to solve your financial headaches.

The Motley Fool UK **http://fool.co.uk**
These are the guys that helped start the whole online share mania, now in the UK. Clear reports and information to debunk the myths and prove that professionals aren't always right. Very active discussion groups let you natter about your top tips.

The Treasury **www.hm-treasury.gov.uk**
What's happening to tax and interest rates? Find out from the official UK government site on budgets and economic indicators.

This Is Money **www.thisismoney.com**
The inescapable truth about life, death and taxes. Great for money newbies with clear but realistic news and features.

Insurance

Car Quote **www.carquote.co.uk**
Fill in the online forms and you'll get car insurance quotes emailed or posted to you from a range of suppliers.

Home Quote UK **http://home.quote.co.uk**
Fill in your details and you'll get house insurance quotes from half a dozen companies.

Screen Trade **www.screentrade.co.uk**

Reduce your insurance by comparing umpteen different suppliers – for car, house and travel.

Mortgages

There are strict UK regulations that govern selling mortgages, and so far just a couple of lenders let you apply for a loan online. However, try these lenders for planners, gizmos to help calculate how much you can borrow and, if you can't apply online, a phone number to make an appointment at your local branch.

Abbey National	**www.abbeynational.co.uk**
Alliance & Leicester	**www.alliance-leicester.co.uk**
Royal Bank of Scotland	**www.bankofscotland.co.uk**
Bradford & Bingley	**www.bradford-bingley.co.uk**
Bristol & West	**www.bristol-west.co.uk**
Cheltenham & Gloucester	**www.cheltglos.co.uk**
Direct Line	**www.directline.com**
Egg	**www.egg.com**
e-loan	**www.eloan.com**
Halifax	**www.halifax.co.uk**
Nationwide	**www.nationwide.co.uk**
Northern Rock	**www.nrock.co.uk**
Virgin Direct	**www.virgin-direct.co.uk**

Pensions

You can't apply for a pension online and for the best advice you should discuss your pension plans and financial future with an independent financial advisor (IFA) – you can find your nearest using FIND (**www.find.co.uk**) or MoneyExtra (**www.moneyextra.co.uk**). Most of the major banks offer pensions (see page 108), or look at this selection of the best-known pension companies:

Equitable Life **www.equitable.co.uk**
Prudential **www.pru.co.uk**
Scottish Widows **www.scottishwidows.co.uk**
Standard Life **www.standardlife.co.uk**
Sun Life **www.slocpensions.co.uk**

//BEAUTY

For the best range of make-up, perfumes and beauty products at the lowest prices, you cannot beat the web. You can get every shade of lipstick, nail varnish and blusher, from local to exotic brands – at low prices. Perfumes are available at less than you'd pay in duty free and you can source exclusive hair and beauty treatments from around the world and have them delivered straight to your door.

Avon Cosmetics **www.avon.com**
Don't wait for the lady to ding-dong on the doorbell, browse and buy online from this slick site.

Body Herbals **www.body-herbals.com**
Herbal shampoos, make-up, moisturisers and bath products that haven't been tested on animals.

Clinique **www.clinique.com**
Choose the perfect lipstick. Although it only concentrates on its own range of cosmetic products there's plenty of helpful information about choosing and using make-up and skincare products.

DSM's Discount Perfume for Women **http://a1.com/dsm/perfume.html**
Cunning chemists have come up with near identical versions of top perfumes – and you can buy them here at cut price.

Easyshop **www.easyshop.co.uk**
Perfume – lots of it – plus tights, undies and bras at discount prices. All the usual major brand names. Easy to use, friendly to shop in.

Fragrance Counter **www.fragrancecounter.com**
Vast range of smells to suit him and her. You won't save much money, but they ship around the world.

FragranceNet **www.fragrancenet.com**
Similar to Fragrance Counter and a couple of bucks cheaper for the main brands.

HQ Hair Products **www.hqhair.co.uk**
Have a lowlite colour weave, buy from a good range of haircare brands (Redken, Paul Mitchell, Fudge) or ask Jayne, their stylist, questions by email.

Lookfantastic **www.lookfantastic.com**
Beauty salon with impressive discounts on styling, conditioners, treatments, skincare, shampoo and even hairdryers.

Marlene Klein Cosmetics **www.marleneklein.com**
You won't find this range of US cosmetics or make-up anywhere except the Internet – so nice Marlene can sell them more cheaply than the brand name equivalents.

Perfume Garden **www.perfume-world.co.uk**
Reasonable selection of perfumes – none from Chanel; more Estée Lauder and Elizabeth Arden.

Personal Care **www.personalcare.co.uk**
Shave and groom with goods from the giant UK mall.

//BOOKS AND MAGAZINES

Books represent a great commodity for the web. You don't need to hold inventory and you can slash prices and ship out with minimal effort. It takes very little time or investment to set up an online bookshop with a vast range of titles on offer and as a result there are hundreds of bookshops online. It's also great news for the consumer: you can browse reviews, read sample chapters and order hard-to-find titles with very little effort.

The spectacular success of Amazon.com has made its founder Jeff Bezos a multi-billionaire and inspired a whole gang of copycat hopefuls. Lots of the smaller sites are trying to get in on the action by selling specialist books on particular subject areas. The market has now reached an unstable balance of power with two levels. First, the big guys all list the same astonishing number of titles (about 1.4 million for UK shops), offer deep discounts (around 50% for bestsellers) and lots of features like reader reviews, ratings and charts.

The second level carries the specialist shops that dig around for hard-to-find titles and add value with news, reports and stories – much like an old local bookshop. The best shopping solution is to take advantage of both: when you want a bestseller, use ShopSmart (**www.shopsmart.com**) or Taxi (**www. mytaxi.co.uk**) to search across all the big bookshops for the cheapest price. When you want something unusual, out of print or technical, go for a specialist shop.

General books

101cd.com **www.101cd.com**

A great range of CDs, videos, DVDs and computer games – and a few books. All at discount prices. Includes reviews and staff recommendations.

Alphabetstreet Books UK **www.alphabetstreet.co.uk**
One of the nicest, cheapest UK-based online booksellers.

Amazon.com **www.amazon.co.uk**
This is the one that started it all, and it is still the market leader. However, the rivals are catching up quickly: Barnes & Noble has a wider selection and local UK shops have better prices. There are also plenty of price differences between the US and UK versions of the shop – prices are often lower in the US edition (Amazon.com) and it now includes everything from the kitchen sink to videos, music CDs and gifts for sale, whereas the UK edition (Amazon.co.uk) sticks to books, videos, CDs and DVDs.

Barnes & Noble **www.bn.com**
The online bookshop equivalent of the great US chain now offers the widest range of books on the net. There's even Starbucks coffee for sale (B&N bought the company), software, out-of-print titles and magazines.

Blackwells Bookshop **http://bookshop.blackwell.co.uk**
The high-street shop with an academic bent provides plenty of high- and lowbrow books for sale. There are very few discounts, but you do get free postage and similar offers. The full search feature lets you hunt for titles by publication date or by other bibliographic details.

BOL **www.uk.bol.com**
The newest of the mega online bookshops; some nice features (such as your own bookshelf of favourite books). Not always as reliable as the other big sites, though. To make Euro-visitors feel at home, there are different localised sites for the major European countries.

Books.com **www.books.com**
You've read it, now chat about it. An online bookseller whose strength is its great range of interactive forums where you can discuss books.

Bookstore.co.uk **www.bookstore.co.uk**
Books, videos and software from around the world are listed here. It's a pretty basic shop design, and there are friendlier places to buy.

BookZone **www.bookzone.co.uk**
Clear site without a mass of special offers and text, just the usual vast range of books, plus videos and CDs. Minimal descriptions and non-bestsellers are only listed by title and ISBN but, if you know what you want, it's efficient.

Borders **www.borders.com**
Vast bookshop chain, provides masses of choice with good service.

countrybookstore.co.uk **www.countrybookstore.co.uk**
Over a million titles listed, together with a good out-of-print locator and impressive discounts.

Heffers **www.heffers.co.uk**
Plenty of choice from a good-looking site that has reviews from the papers, special offers and recommendations. Just a single click adds an item to your shopping basket, so be careful.

The Book People **www.thebookpeople.co.uk**
Excellent site that's doing battle by discounting furiously. At the time of writing, every other shop had just discounted to 50% – these folk were on to 75%.

The Book Pl@ce **www.thebookplace.com**
Nice shop with the usual massive range of books, plus videos and CDs. The site is good on customer support – with names and phone numbers – and your order is actually processed by Hammicks, the high-street shop.

The Internet Book Shop **www.bookshop.co.uk**
Now owned by WH Smith, there's the standard selection of over 1.4 million titles plus CDs, videos and games. Friendly cyber-clerk Jenny

will keep you up to date with new titles as they are published. Decent offers to match the other big guns but without the reviews of Amazon.

Waterstones **www.waterstones.co.uk**
Lots of choice in a smart-looking, easy-to-navigate site. You can exchange any book by nipping in to your local Waterstones shop. Lots of savings and reader reviews.

Specialist books

American Technical Publishers Ltd **www.ameritech.co.uk**
Textbooks, academic CDs and videos from non-UK publishers. Search and order online. No great shakes on presentation, but that suits the job.

Books for Children **http://freespace.virgin.net/books-for.children/**
A real-life bookshop in London that's slowly coming online – a small selection of key titles, but they'll find anything if you send them a friendly email.

Children's Book Centre **www.childrensbookcentre.co.uk**
Modest selection of titles and with a few pictures, but neatly arranged by age group and with good descriptions.

Computer Manuals Online Bookstore **www.compman.co.uk**
The largest specialist computer book supplier in the UK has packed the entire range into this sombre site, but there are very good discounts.

High Stakes Gambling Bookshop **www.highstakes.co.uk**
Great selection of books about gambling. No frills, just the books and the most basic details.

Funorama **www.funorama.com**
Lots to read, do and colour in with reviews of books by subject and age.

Maps Worldwide **www.mapsworldwide.co.uk**
Over 10,000 maps of the world – from street-level to global. Plenty of discounts and free shipping in the UK on orders over £5.00.

OKUKBooks **www.okukbooks.com**
Jolly, fun place to read about and buy children's books. Reviews by children and a friendly style make it a nice place to shop.

Sportpages **www.sportspages.co.uk**
Thousands of books and videos on sport – easy to use, nice design and lots of information to help you choose.

Virgin Books **www.virgin-books.com**
Discount prices on sport, travel, music, and erotic books from the people who brought you this essential volume.

Watkins **www.watkinsbooks.com**
Over 40,000 books and music on mind-body-spirit subjects plus religions, mythology and occult. Unfortunately, there's little in the way of descriptions to help you make a choice.

Old books

Bibliofind **www.bibliofind.com**
Amazon-owned search engine that indexes over 2,000 antiquarian booksellers (mostly from the US, but they can deliver).

BookLovers **www.booklovers.co.uk**
Buy or sell secondhand books – decent selection with plenty of first editions; online ordering and links for book lovers.

International bookshops

Can't find it locally? Buy from some of the biggest and slickest online stores around the world:

Chapters **www.chapters.ca**
The biggest bookshop chain in Canada.

Dymocks **www.dymocks.com.au**
Australia's finest bookshop stores.

Magazines

British Magazines Direct **www.britishmagazines.com**
Thousands of UK magazines available direct from this online newsagent. Easy to use, and a few discounts.

Magazine Shop **www.magazineshop.co.uk**
Subscribe to any of the 475 UK magazines listed. There are some discounts, but you might find it's cheaper via an in-mag promotion.

//BUSINESS AND BUSINESSES

Instead of phoning for your stationery, order it direct from the website of any of the large suppliers – there are even a few extra discounts and offers to tempt web customers (though not enough). For the other office essentials, look to the computer section for hardware and software and to the electrical section for air-conditioning, kettles and microwaves. And if you want to buy a business, the classified-ad magazines make it easy to spot the perfect opportunity.

Office supplies

Ashfields **www.ashfields.com**
Furnish your office or reception with a good range of desks, chairs and sofas.

Biztravel.com **www.biztravel.com**
The top travel site for jet-setting business types. This US service supports UK customers and lets you track frequent flyer schemes, book planes, hotels and cars. It even records your preferences for seats and meals.

Exchange and Mart **www.exchangeandmart.co.uk**
Business classifieds – from business equipment to businesses.

Laser Clarity **www.laserclarity.com**
Design your own business cards – easy steps, but at £44 for 50, it's pretty expensive.

Neat Ideas **www.neat-ideas.com**
Rival to Viking puts up a great fight online.

Roadnews.com **www.roadnews.com**
You've landed in LA, your laptop's at the ready and you realise you've forgotten the adapter to connect your modem to the phone. This site helps out with news, tips and supplier listings for batteries, connectors and more. Trouble is, if you can't connect to the web, how do you access the site?

The Office Shop **www.owa.co.uk**
Staplers to printers, paper pads to PCs – at low prices.

Viking Direct **www.viking-direct.co.uk**
The office bible now online; try rival Neat Ideas for a similar range and pricing.

Yellow Pages

Everyone uses the Yellow Pages – now it's online and fully indexed; great for business to business or personal users who want to find a business.

Australia	**www.yellowpages.com.au**
Canada	**www.canadayellowpages.com**
Ireland	**www.nci.ie/yellow/**
New Zealand	**www.yellowpages.co.nz**
South Africa	**www.easyinfo.co.za**
UK	**www.yell.co.uk**
USA	**www.bigyellow.com**

Businesses

Daltons **www.daltons.co.uk**
Buy a pub or get a franchise from the weekly classified magazine listing business opportunities, premises, franchises and other deals.

Exchange and Mart **www.exchangeandmart.co.uk**
Business classifieds – from business equipment to businesses.

Moore, Wood & Cockram **www.mwclicproperty.demon.co.uk**
Buy a pub or restaurant from this specialist company that deals in nothing else.

//CAMERAS

There are surprisingly few sites dedicated to cameras – but luckily, the few are very good! Instead, you'll find cheap cameras are now as accessories in leisure, electrical or computer shops. Unlike other specialist shops on the high street there does not seem to have been a rush online from those selling cameras. This in marked contrast to the end product – without photographs, the web would be a very dull place. The Euro Foto Centre superstore is one of the main exceptions – it sells everything from darkroom equipment to tripods. However, the biggest store on the web, AccessCamera (**www.accesscamera.com**), is in the USA and currently won't ship abroad.

Camera **www.camera.com**
Reasonable choice at low US prices – not the range of market leaders AccessCamera, but they will at least ship around the world.

Cameras Direct **www.camerasdirect.co.uk**
Video, compact, digital and conventional big-name cameras and equipment – online and at a discount.

Euro Foto Centre **www.euro-foto.com**
Huge range of video, photographic, darkroom equipment, accessories and materials.

Digital Camera Company **www.digital-cameras.com**
The best range of digital cameras. Great descriptions, general advice and accessories – but no online ordering yet.

Dixons **www.dixons.co.uk**
Everything that's for sale in the high-street store is available online – including a reasonable range of traditional, digital and video.

KEH **www.keh.com**
Not much in the way of descriptive text or pictures, but a truly vast range of used cameras, lenses and accessories. Ships from the US around the world.

Marriott Photo & Cine **www.marriott.u-net.com**
Classic – but very useable – still and cine cameras; order online via a rather basic order form.

Photo Forum **www.photoforum.co.uk**

Good range of film and digital cameras and film – plus guides to choosing and using the kit. Part of the vast Shoppers Universe mall.

Photoshopper Online **www.photoshopper.com**

Collection of dealer-based products, classifieds and swap-meets that provide a busy place to look for cameras and accessories – but, so far, this US site hasn't installed secure ordering.

Simply Scuba **www.simplyscuba.co.uk**

Snorkels, flippers – and underwater cameras.

Unbeatable **www.unbeatable.co.uk**

Good prices for camcorders and cameras.

//CARS

Why not buy your next car on the web? It's easy to carry out exhaustive research, find the best price, check availability and even haggle by email. The Internet has already started to revolutionize the car-buying process, with great benefits for consumers across the range. If you're looking for a secondhand estate or want to save on a new model, the web can help.

None of these sites actually provides a shopping basket to let you buy a car online, but they'll make it very easy to choose and find the car you want at the right price. The large magazine-style review sites provide news and reviews of models and makes and many let you do your own tests and compare two different models on features and price. Once you've decided on a make and model, you can use one of the new car search sites such as Auto-By-Tel and New Car Network to link to distributors around the country to find the best car at the lowest price.

For secondhand cars, the classified listing papers *AutoTrader* and *Exchange and Mart* dominate. Both have searchable databases that enable you to find cars to your exact spec and within a convenient drive from home anytime. Better still, set up an email alert and you'll be the first to hear when an ad for your perfect car is placed.

Autobytel **www.autobytel.co.uk**
Hunt for a new or used car via an extensive dealer network.

AutoExpress **www.autoexpress.co.uk**
Every tiny detail about the latest thing on four wheels. Car-crazy web addicts can wallow in the vast database of road tests, check prices and browse the classifieds (though *AutoTrader* and *Exchange and Mart* are bigger). Use the Links button to get a directory of the websites for all the major car manufacturers.

AutoTrader **www.autotrader.co.uk**
Search the thousands of classifieds in an instant – or get an email when someone advertises your dream car. On a par with arch-rival *Exchange and Mart*.

Carsource **www.carsource.co.uk**
Azure blue, tinted glass, alloys and air-con? Use the search system that matches your requirements with new and used cars available from main dealers. Once you've found the car, there are links to insurance companies, lease and finance groups. For used cars, you'll get a better range from *AutoTrader* and *Exchange and Mart*.

Classic Car Monthly **www.classicmotor.co.uk**
Find a spare bumper for your Spitfire or a gasket for the Minor. A great site for classic car owners who want to get spares, advice, talk to other owners or show off their cars. And if you're under pressure to sell the pride and joy (or box of bits), there are listings for autojumbles.

Classic Cars Source **www.classicar.com**
The shiniest chrome-plated site for classic car enthusiasts. This US

site provides a wealth of information on marques, events, spares, clubs and cars for sale.

Exchange and Mart **www.exchangeandmart.co.uk**

All the classified ads without hunting through the magazine. A simple search function and an email update will ensure you're the first to hear about a new entry. On a par with *AutoTrader* (www.autotrader.co.uk).

Fish4Cars **www.fish4cars.co.uk**

Helps you find a car from the UK's local papers.

Haynes shop **www.haynes.co.uk**

It's Sunday evening, the shops are closed, the engine's in pieces and you don't know what you're doing. When this site first launched, you could buy and download a book – a great idea. Now, you can only buy the printed product sent through the post.

MotoringClassics **www.motoringclassics.com**

One of the best sites for great old cars for sale.

New Car Net **www.new-car-net.co.uk**

Help choosing your new car. Enter your basic criteria, then compare the models and read in-depth reviews on each. Links to your nearest specialist dealer to complete the deal.

Parker's **www.parkers.co.uk**

The best place to find the true price of any used car.

Virgin Cars **www.virgincars.co.uk**

Beats down the EU barriers and supplies low-price cars to the UK.

Virtual Showroom **www.virtualshowroom.co.uk**

An index of (mostly used) cars available from dealers around the UK. Nothing fancy and you'll see a better selection with the top two classified magazines (*AutoTrader* and *Exchange and Mart*).

WhatCar? **www.whatcar.co.uk**
A little of everything car-related has been crammed into this informative site. The main features are the road tests but there's also classifieds, used car prices, insurance and finance features.

//CHOCOLATES AND SWEETS

OK, you're never going to use the Internet to buy your teatime Mars Bar or Twix, but there are dozens of chocolate suppliers online – with the finest (generally Belgian) handmade chocs to tempt the strongest will. Keep up to date with their regular choco email bulletins, then crumble and order a kilo. Some of the suppliers are in the US, but they ship direct and, in the summer months, include a cool pad to keep the goodies from melting into the FedEx pack.

AusomeCandies.com **www.ausomecandies.com**
Lolly and gum maker sells cut-price sweeties – but you'll need a gang of kids: they only sell in box-loads.

Bogdon's Candies **www.bogdonschocolates.com**
Flavoured sticks dipped in dark chocolate – if you've had them, you'll love them.

Candy Direct **www.candydirect.com**
Top site for sweets.

ChocExpress **www.chocexpress.co.uk**
Plenty of chocs and a choc-chooser – tell them about the person and it will choose a suitable box.

Chocolate Society **www.chocolate.co.uk**
Pure indulgence.

Chocolatestore.com **www.chocolatestore.com**
Handmade chocs, truffles and personalised champagne gifts.

Nirvana Chocolates **www.nirvanachocolates.com**

Indulge your passion by customising your selection of handmade Belgian chocolates.

//CLOTHING

Perhaps because consumers are used to buying clothes in catalogues, this is one of the great areas for the Internet shopper. There are an amazing number of clothes shops, manufacturers and distributors with secure online ordering. From chic evening dresses to cheap cotton shirts, you'll find the range is staggering. The big-name suppliers generally offer extra discounts or free goodies (such as a free T-shirt) when you order online, but the Internet really comes into its own with specialist shops supplying boxer shorts, custom-made swimming costumes, vast ranges of undies and bras, handmade suits, shoes and shirts.

Action Fit **www.actionfit.com**

Design your own swimsuit.

America's Shirt Catalog **www.hugestore.com**

Huge range of top US clothes at discount prices. With discounts of up to 40%, clear navigation and plenty of good pix make it easy to shop.

Aaargh Fashions **www.aaargh.co.uk**

Racy undies (what, you hadn't guessed from the name?) made in everything from lace to rubber.

Best of British **www.thebestofbritish.com**

Nothing kitsch and few Union Jacks – just a great range of top-quality brands (Molton Brown, Mulberry, Lulu Guiness) covering fashion, food and home – plenty of discounts and nice presentation.

Birkenstock Express On-line **www.footwise.com**
Love them or loathe them, this site has a great range of these cult sandals and shoes at low prices. They can be coaxed to ship out of the US and there's even a repair service if your Birks break.

Boden **www.boden.co.uk**
Elegant clothes for men, women and children from this slick mail-order supplier.

Bras Direct **www.brasdirect.co.uk**
Browse thousands of bra shapes, styles and sizes. A friendly virtual assistant helps with advice on fitting. And, please, no jokes about customer support.

Brooks Brothers **www.brooksbrothers.com**
Elegant preppy classics from upmarket US label – blazers, smart casuals and suits – for him and her. They'll ship overseas, but for small items the postal costs are very high.

Burtons Menswear **www.burtonmenswear.co.uk**
Men's clothes from the British high-street giant plus related shops Hawkshead and TopMan – a good-looking site that's given a new-man spin with football and fashion themes.

Cafe Coton **www.cafecoton.co.uk**
Pure-cotton French-style shirts for weekends and office days (though for formal double-cuff styles you'll have to try Thyrwitt).

Charles Thyrwitt **www.ctshirts.co.uk**
Smart shirts in every size imaginable – plus ties, cufflinks, braces and other essentials. A very clear site design makes this super-easy to use.

Christian Scott **www.christianscott.com**
Scottish cashmere and wool throws, jackets, scarves and rugs are available from this Aberdeen-based mill.

City Boxers **www.cityboxers.com**
Boxer shorts in plaids, prints, colours, cartoons and flannel. And absolutely no greying saggy Y-fronts.

Clothing Connection **www.clothingconnection.co.uk**
A large online mall that includes Lingerie Label (all the main names) and Clothing Connection for men and women's everyday wear – or high-fashion clothes and even children's clothes. A good place to start but, like all malls, you'll find a better selection in individual specialist shops.

Cow Town Boots **www.cowtownboots.com**
Stride around in the finest cowboy boots direct from the makers in El Paso: there's rattlesnake, ostrich and python to choose from. You'll have to phone Texas for the latest rates on shipping.

Diesel UK Virtual Store **www.diesel.co.uk**
More than just denim from the trendy designers. Cool design, few offers but plenty of street-style for both men and women including jeans, shirts, jackets and much more. Great presentation and easy to navigate.

Dollond and Aitchison Sunglasses **www.dollond.co.uk**
There's no mirror but you can scan in your photo and drag the specs on to it to see how cool you really look.

Dorothy Perkins **www.dorothyperkins.co.uk**
Fine transition from high street to website; provides quick-shop facility or a leisurely browse through the racks of evening, business, casual and maternity wear. A few online special offers.

Easyshop **www.easyshop.co.uk**
Tights, undies, bras and perfume – lots of perfume – at discount prices that include delivery. You'll find the usual major brand names. Easy to use, friendly to shop in.

Edward Teach **www.edward-teach.com**
Good savings of 20% off a range of high-quality off-the-peg or made-to-measure clothes and shoes. Includes Crombie, Haggar, Bjorn Borg and Alfred Sargent.

Esprit **www.esprit-intl.com**
Stylish, minimalist women's clothes from the west coast of the US. Great-looking site and items and a European-specific section to make life easier when ordering.

Fabric8 **www.fabric8.com/sg/fit_1.html**
Wild and funky site, and clothes, from some of the coolest street designers around. Best of all is the great virtual trickery that measures and cuts to fit exactly.

FADE Fashion **www.fade-fashion.com**
A modest selection of golfing and casual gear, from chinos to polo shirts.

Fashionmall.com **www.fashionmall.com**
A central mall to browse a wide range of clothes stores, from D&G to Liz Claiborne. A good place to start looking for clothes, but it's weak on beauty products.

Fat Face Online Store **www.fatface.co.uk**
Surf-world hits web-world with the funky range of outdoor and sports fleeces and shirts for the family. Online shoppers earn Fat Calories that'll add up to a 10% discount.

Freemans **www.freemans.com**
Includes all the items from the famous catalogue – Ralph Lauren to Betty Jackson, Levi to Caterpillar. No special web offers, but you do get free delivery.

Global Caps **www.globalcaps.com**
Hundreds of baseball cap designs on offer.

Harvie and Hudson www.harvieandhudson.com
Fine tradition seeps from every corner of this nicely designed site. Order your trad shirts and ties here – or get them made to measure. There's also a discount scheme for repeat customers.

Henry & June www.henryandjune.com
Wonderful selection of romantic lingerie – and a great returns guarantee.

Highland Dress Online www.highland-dress.co.uk
Get fitted for a kilt or sporran – order the full kit or individual pieces of authentic Scottish dress in over 1,200 patterns. And there's a handy list to help you work out which clan you're in.

IC3D Jeans www.ic3d.com
Custom-made jeans from New York. Send them measurements or even your favourite pair of jeans and they will produce the best-fitting denim you've ever worn. It's a complex site (you've got to give a lot of measurements and there are more than 120 fabrics to choose from).

IntoFashion www.intofashion.com
Quirky, trendy clothes – from Jasper Conran and the like – in a bright, stylish UK shop.

Jones Bootmaker www.jonesbootmaker.com
Fine footwear for men and women: work, play or evening shoes. There are a few online special offers and free delivery.

Kays www.kaysnet.com
The online version of the vast Kays home-shopping catalogue. Over 25,000 products and free home delivery. Piles of good-quality items in fashion, toys, DIY and sports.

Kiniki www.kiniki.com
Top thongs for your main man – designer boxers, undies and swimwear.

Lands' End **www.landsend.com**
The company behind basic cotton clothes has one of the coolest website features around – a virtual model you can tailor to your size, shape and hair colouring before you dress it up.

La Redoute **www.redoute.co.uk**
Cool, elegant French clothes.

L.L. Bean **www.llbean.com**
Famed outdoor clothing supplier – from checked shirts to hunting boots – a super-slick site that keeps winning awards.

Metropolis Clothing **www.metropolis-clothing.com**
Top-name clothes at great prices – the site itself looks functional but the labels and prices are anything but. Send in a snap of yourself wearing the clothes to get a fiver back in return.

Paul Smith **www.paulsmith.co.uk**
High fashion meets the high street with a fusion of sound and images from this classy designer's range of clothes.

Principles **www.principles.co.uk**
Masses of good-looking clothes for women presented with plenty of pictures and information in a smartly turned-out site that's easy to use.

Racing Green **www.racinggreen.co.uk**
Smart casual gear for men and women – from polo tops to flowery dresses. Few discounts but there are competitions and similar specials.

Sax Design **www.saxdesign.com**
Fine silk ties printed with a whole range of pictures and images – from computer geeky PCs to fruity apples and pear, all at the ex-factory prices.

Scotia **www.scotia.uk.com**
Perfect gear for the UK outdoors – Barbour and Musto waterproofs

and a small, select range of other clothes. No discounts or web specials, however.

Shipton & Heneage **www.shiphen.com**
Smart, traditional UK bench-made shoes, boots and slippers for gents and ladies. Excellent photographs and a clear site design make shopping simple.

ShopLine **www.shopline.co.uk**
Braces, ties and cufflinks emblazoned with cartoon, sporting and drinking motifs.

Skinzwear **www.skinzwear.com**
Amazing (and skintight) swimsuits and active gear that only the confident, or beautiful, can wear.

The Clothes Store **www.the-clothes-store.com**
Street-wise chic men's clothing including Ben Sherman, Fred Perry, Lee and Dr Martens. Clean, simple site design makes it easy to navigate the impressive range of shirts, shoes and trousers.

The GAP **www.gap.com**
You know the stuff – basic cotton chinos, T's and polo shirts – exactly like in the shopping centre, but without the crowds.

The Shirt Press **www.shirt-press.co.uk**
Pure cotton shirts that – astonishingly – never need to be ironed. Miracles can happen.

T-shirt King **www.t-shirtking.com**
From Scooby-doo to South Park, you'll find hundreds of officially licensed T-shirts for sale ready to ship out around the world.

US Cavalry **www.uscav.com**
Vietnam combat boots, camouflage gear, plus all the accessories to look and feel like a mercenary. Not really for the office, but just the thing to wear when paintballing.

Victoria's Secret **www.victoriassecret.com**
The full range of world-famous undies modelled by astonishingly pretty girls. For men, see Kiniki.

Zercon **www.zercon.com**
Top designer threads at low, low prices.

//COMPUTERS

No prizes for guessing that there are plenty of computer shops online – selling software, computers and accessories. The discounts are great and the range amazing. Most of the large superstores now sell everything from a PC to software, modems to laptops, games to CDs. Many computer manufacturers let you build your own custom computer in their online shops (see the box for these companies). We've divided this section into hardware (modems and cables), software (the applications) and games (for PCs and consoles). However, more than in any other section, you'll find each supplier tries to provide everything you need to feed your computing habit, so there's plenty of crossover.

US computer suppliers

You'll find the US home to some of the keenest prices and sharpest discounts on new hardware and software. However, if you don't live in the US, beware since many warranties and guarantees rarely extend outside the country of purchase, so check with manufacturer first. If you're willing to risk this, then you'll normally have to arrange and pay for repairs through a local repair company.

Software

Beyond.com **www.beyond.com**
Cyberian Outpost **www.outpost.com**

BookMark Software	**www.bookmarksoftware.com**
Chumbo.com	**www.chumbo.com**
Egghead.com	**www.egghead.com**

Hardware

Computers4sure	**www.computers4sure.com**
Cyberian Outpost	**www.outpost.com**
eGames:	**www.egames.com**
Egghead.com	**www.egghead.com**
NECX	**www.necx.com**
NetBuyer	**www.netbuyer.com**

Custom-built computers

Apple Store	**www.apple.com**
DELL	**www.dell.co.uk**
Elonex	**www.elonex.co.uk**
Evesham Micros	**www.evesham.com**
Gateway 2000	**www.gw2k.com**
Tiny	**www.tiny.co.uk**
Viglen	**www.viglen.co.uk**

Computer hardware

Action Computer Supplies **www.action.com**
Business-orientated hardware, software and accessories supplier. Great service, good prices and a site that's informative and easy to use.

CD Revolution **www.cdrevolution.com**
Stop by for a good range of CD recording drives and media.

CommStore **www.commstore.co.uk**
Everything to get you connected – modems, ISDN adapters, routers and Internet software.

Crab Chemical **www.inkjet-service.co.uk**

Refill kits for your ink-jet. Do it yourself and save up to 80% of the cost of a new replacement cartridge.

Dabs Direct **www.dabs.com**

Good range of hardware and software from top names at low prices – with free delivery thrown in. Could do with more technical info about the products, though.

Dixons **www.dixons.co.uk**

Anything that's for sale in the high-street store is available online – that means TVs, hi-fi systems, PCs, fax machines and cameras.

Inmac **www.inmac.co.uk**

Well-stocked warehouse piled high with hardware and software at low prices and with great service.

Insight **www.insight.com/uk/**

Over 40,000 top-brand names on the virtual shelves. Good prices and next-day delivery, but you'll need to know what you're after before you visit.

Jungle.com **www.jungle.com**

Smart shop packed with hardware, software, music and videos at low prices.

Microwarehouse **www.microwarehouse.co.uk**

Provides just about the best range of computer hardware, software and accessories at good prices.

Misco **www.misco.co.uk**

Cables to printers, there's heaps of computer hardware in store.

Morgan Computer **www.morgancomputers.co.uk**

Cheap and cheerful end-of-line or used brand name computers, printers and other office equipment.

Network Solutions **www.network-solutions.co.uk**
Everything to build, then trouble-shoot, your network. Impressive design makes it one of the easiest sites to navigate.

Pico Direct **www.picodirect.co.uk**
Portable computers – and that's it. Shop from the range of brand name goods and its own line of laptops.

RS Components **www.rswww.com**
Specialist electronic and computing supplier. The place to go if you're looking for a connector, chip, cable, widget or thingammy.

Simply Computers **www.simply.co.uk**
Good range of hardware and software includes all the main brands and their own line of PCs.

TechWeb **www.techweb.com/shopper**
Comprehensive database of computer hardware and software that will help you decide what's best for you.

Computer software

CD Direct **www.cddirect.co.uk**
Excellent range of software on CD – from games to office-application CDs. Easy navigation, good budget titles and plenty of reviews.

Dixons **www.dixons.co.uk**
Bright, gawdy site selling a small selection of PC and console games along with all the other electrical goods from the high-street shop.

Download.com **www.download.com**
Great library of commercial-application software and shareware that you can buy and instantly download to your computer – part of the impressive CNET resource site.

ECHO Software **www.echosoftware.com**
Masses of second-user software plus over 100,000 software titles to buy and download directly to your computer.

eShop **www.eshop.co.uk**
Heavy on the programming and Internet titles, but there's also general home-user sections.

PC World Software **www.pcw-software.co.uk**
If you can't find your local PC World, this site lists their full range of over 2,000 titles. Easy to navigate, but look to Software Paradise for cheaper, wider selections.

Software Paradise **www.softwareparadise.co.uk**
Over 100,000 software titles for sale at discount prices. Covers all platforms from PC to Mac – and from developers around the world.

Software Savings **www.softwaresavings.co.uk**
Modest range of software (mostly applications) at knock-down prices.

Software Station **www.softwarestation.co.uk**
Bestselling software for PCs and games consoles. Very simple to navigate and part of the Shoppers Universe shopping mall.

Software Warehouse **www.software-warehouse.co.uk**
Extensive range of software and peripherals – providing reviews of each product, all the brand names at low prices and, in some cases, instant download.

The Educational Software Company **www.educational.co.uk**
Over 1,000 of the top educational software programs at reasonable prices. The recommendations help you pick the right program for your child's age and level.

Tucows **www.tucows.com**
Great range of techie shareware and demos to boost Windows, your website or browsing experience.

Computer games

101cd.com **www.101cd.com**
A half-million catalogue list that carries games (and books, DVDs, and videos, too). Add your own review to any entry or pre-order forthcoming releases.

CD Direct **www.cddirect.co.uk**
Good range for all platforms, plenty of reviews, promotions and budget titles – plus you can pre-order forthcoming titles to make sure you're the first to get a copy.

Entertainment Express **www.entexpress.com**
Plenty of choice and nice to shop in, but prices of the games, music and videos are on a par with the high street.

Game **www.game-retail.co.uk**
Total gaming overload. Reviews, news, charts, product information – and all the games and accessories you could want.

Games and Videos **www.gamesandvideos.com**
More emphasis on the videos than the games, but still stocks a respectable 4,000 titles for all platforms.

Games Paradise **www.gamesparadise.com**
Part of WH Smith, this site sells games for all computers and consoles at low prices. Includes charts, reviews and product details.

HMV **www.hmv.co.uk**
Modest selection from the high-street giant, but there are reviews, offers and information to tempt you in.

Nintendo Direct **www.nintendodirect.co.uk**
Wallow in vast troughs of charts, news and reviews before browsing heaving shelves stacked high with games for N64.

PlayStation Direct **www.playstationdirect.co.uk**
From the clever company that set up Nintendo Direct – another winning specialist shop.

Special Reserve **www.reserve.co.uk**
Just about the cheapest, widest range of computer games available. And, if you're still deciding, there's reviews and gaming news.

UK Games **www.ukgames.com**
Packed with demos, news, tips, cheats, charts – and, of course, the latest and greatest games at low prices.

URwired **www.urwired.com**
Low prices for the latest games for PC, PlayStation and Nintendo. Unusually, prices already include delivery.

Lots In Store **www.lotsinstore.com**
Plenty of reviews and news help you choose new games for your console.

Visions Online **www.visionsonline.co.uk**
Swap your game for another. Bored with Lara? Exchange games software for PlayStation, Nintendo and Sega Saturn platforms.

//CRAFTS

From fine silverwork to needlework, there are specialist shops online that sell the work of artisans or the equipment you need to do it yourself. Many of the craft sites provide help, advice and communities to exchange ideas and tips; some include galleries to help sell your work. Professional online craft galleries are often easier to deal with, but they are more expensive. And have a look at the artist materials and hobby sections of the directory for shops that supply related areas.

Cass Arts **www.cass-arts.co.uk**
Everything you need to create your masterpiece – over 10,000 art and craft products in store, plus tips, advice and step-by-step lessons to get you started.

Country Crafts **www.countrycrafts.co.uk**
UK artisans producing a wide range of gifts and ornaments – jewellery, hats, paintings and pottery. Part of BarclaySquare.

Country Sampler **www.countrysampler.com**
Candles to dolls, woodwork to quilts, you'll find the work of North American country craftspeople available here. Each producer accepts different credit cards and has different shipping procedures – but you're covered by a catch-all 30-day guarantee and right to return. Plus there's a magazine and features.

Blue Deco **www.bluedeco.com**
Expensive but beautiful modern work from young designers – covers ceramics, furniture, glassware, metalwork and more.

Crafts Fair Online **www.craftsfaironline.com**
As it says, it's a big crafts fair. You can't really order online – you get directed to the artisan's own (often tiny) website. Still, if you want a handmade bonnet, you know where to find one. Plus there's news, features and crafty discussions.

Empress Mills **www.empressmills.co.uk**
Threads of every colour and type for needlework enthusiasts.

Hobby's **www.hobby.uk.com**
A very modest selection from the company's huge print catalogue dedicated to craft, hobbyist and modelmaker materials.

McDarlins **www.mcdarlins.com**
Order custom calligraphy, beautifully written but rather sentimental set texts or get a custom job. Neat, easy to use with plenty of options, but no mention of returns, guarantees or other customer service stuff.

Sew & So **www.sewandso.co.uk**
Old-fashioned haberdasher and needlework supplier threads into the web with considerable success.

//DEPARTMENT STORES

Dependable, traditional, full of choice – the multi-purpose, multi-department stores might dominate the high street, but it's a different, level playing field on the web. The big names, such as Debenhams and Argos, provide guarantees and a warm, secure feeling as you shop. Virtual malls combine (often rather eclectic) groups of shops that give you a bit of everything. Department stores and malls are good, safe and generally friendly places to start, but you'll soon be exploring outside – there are thousands of specialist shops with wider choices.

Argos **www.argos.co.uk**
Forget the scrap of paper and tiny ballpoint pen, order from the full catalogue of low-priced products.

BarclaySquare **www.barclaysquare.co.uk**
The first and still the best known of the UK malls; its list of specialist stores sells everything from flowers to music, and there's a secure guarantee on any purchase. Very safe, moderately useful but not too easy to navigate.

BrandsforLess.com **www.brandsforless.com**
Vast selection of US discount stores helping save you money, but each of the stores has a different shipping and returns policy for international visitors.

Buckingham Gate **www.buckinghamgate.com**
A Bentley, a teacup or a pair of bespoke shoes, sir? You'll find all three and plenty of other typically UK, if not always still UK-owned, companies in this well-designed site.

Cameron Square **www.cameronsquare.com**
Shopping with a Scottish twist – from Celtic jewellery to smoked salmon.

Catalogues Online **www.couk.co.uk**
Small general department store with a reasonable selection of gifts, clothes and home-style accessories.

Countdown Arcade **www.countdownarcade.com**
Discounts galore for paid-up members of this general department store cum savings club (that costs £49.95 per year to join).

Debenhams **www.debenhams.co.uk**
Everything from the high street department store squeezed neatly on to the web – great design with tempting gift vouchers make it easier to get you shopping on the net.

eDirectory **www.edirectory.co.uk**
The biggest of the UK mall-sites has an impressive 100 shops tucked away, providing more than 250,000 products: software, videos, furniture, clothes, art, books, food and holidays. Phew!

ishop **www.ishop.co.uk**
A decent range of shops with a broad selection of products. Unusually, anyone can (for a price) set up their own niche shop within this site.

JC Penney **www.jcpenney.com**
Giant US department store crashes on to the web – clean, well ordered and with a great selection. They'll happily ship around the world, which rival's Macys (**www.macys.com**) and Nordstrom (**www.nordstrom.com**) won't.

Kays **www.kaysnet.com**
Giant home-shopping catalogue hits the web: includes a vast range from lingerie to DIY. Its rival, Freemans, is also here.

Made in Sheffield **www.made-in-sheffield.com**
Local manufacturers sell their range of cutlery, jewellery and toys. This virtual store also has a real counterpart in the centre of the city if you want to browse in person.

Mersey Mall **www.merseyworld.com/mall/**
Small selection of local shops selling a very odd assortment of goods – from spares for your Land Rover to fashion clothes.

Shoppers Universe **www.shoppersuniverse.com**
One of the better malls around, filled with thousands of brand name items distributed by retail giant Great Universal.

Tesco **www.tesco.co.uk**
Going further than its rival supermarkets, you can order all your food and household products, plus books, music, clothes – even PCs and Internet services.

QVC **www.qvcuk.com**
If you're a fan of the home-shopping TV channel, you'll know what to expect. If not, you can probably guess. In fact, sorted and ordered into sections, it works much better than the shows and, with over 10,000 products, it's one of the bigger shops online.

Shop Yell **www.shopyell.co.uk**
Wide collection of specialist UK shops pulled from the general Yell search directory.

ShoppingCentre **www.shoppingcentre.net**
Great design, reasonable range of books, toys, home-style and health products – and an assistant to help recommend, carry and fetch.

The Virtual Mall **www.thevirtualmall.com**
If you can't be bothered to type in the addresses of well-known stores online, visit this new mall and you'll find them all inside.

//DRINKS AND SMOKES

Twin vices of rack and ruin do well on the net – hunt out fine wine, cheap claret, rare coffee beans or hand-rolled cigars from the specialist suppliers. The biggest suppliers of wine provide shops that inform, keep you up to date and sell; others are rather more up-front and simply list what's in the cellar and how much it costs. Ideally, you want to save money – and you will on cigars and tobacco. Cigarettes are more difficult: the US has vast factory outlets selling off the surplus from Virginia, but in Europe the only discount was closed down due to EU laws.

Buy wine online and you're likely to save with the specialists, but the online versions of high-street shops don't discount (though you might get free delivery). But the clinching argument for shopping for either is the vast range available, and the fact you don't have to lug vast crates of liquor around.

Alcoholic drinks

Beers Direct **www.beersdirect.com**
Sit down, feet-up, login and order crates of your favourite brews, delivered to your door. Good prices include delivery but the naughty people tell you it's a secure site – it's not.

Berry Bros. & Rudd **www.berry-bros.co.uk**
Wine merchants to the gentry and enthusiast. A clear, informative and addictive site, positively bursting with fine wines.

Black Bottle **www.blackbottle.com**
Blended Islay whisky – nice site, nice drink.

Celebrations Wine Club **www.celebrationswineclub.com**
Wine of the month subscription service giving you reviews and wine from California's leading small-production premium wine makers.

Drinks Direct **www.drinks-direct.co.uk**
Beer and wine by the case, delivered by an offshoot of Thresher.

LastOrders **www.lastorders.com**
Food, music, guests – duh, forgotten the booze. Stacks of wine, beer and spirits ready for delivery.

MadAboutWine **www.madaboutwine.com**
Clear guides and a comprehensive cellar that's stocked with interesting wines at reasonable prices.

Scotch Whisky **www.scotchwhisky.com**
Buy nosing glasses or just read the tasting notes. Sign up (for free) and you can order an impressive range of classic, aged, single malts.

Terroir French Wine **www.terroir.com**
Lots of French wines on offer, with good guides to buying and enjoying what you've just bought.

The Glenturret Distillery **www.glenturret.com**
The oldest distillery in Scotland produces single malts. See how it's made and order a bottle with a personalised label.

The Whisky Shop **www.whiskyshop.com**
Single malt, blended, miniatures, rare – it's got everything. Streaming video gives you a tour of the classics, such as Talisker and Lagavulin, plus you can see a map – or just order.

Virgin Wines **www.virginwines.com**
No idea what you want? Here's a helpful guide to suggest bottles from the online shelves.

Virtual Vineyards **www.virtualvin.com**
Exceptional site for novice wine buffs that tells you all about wine, how to enjoy it and how to choose it – then provides a massive

range of fine wines at reasonable prices that can be shipped around the world.

Wine & Dine **www.winedine.co.uk**

An enjoyable UK monthly magazine from and for wine lovers.

Wine Cellar UK **www.winecellar.co.uk**

Good range of wines (including champagne, fortified and spirits). Plenty of details on each, but the prices are the same as in the high street.

Wine Merchant **www.wine-merchant.com**

Good range of wines from around the world, supplied by the dozen. Fine wines but no descriptions or tasting notes.

WineOnline **www.wineonline.co.uk**

The Brit view on wine tasting, buying and enjoying.

Young's **www.youngs.co.uk/winedirect/**

Beer, wine and spirits from the brewers – decent range with tasting notes, but nothing fine or vintage on the lists. Much like the pubs.

Non-alcoholic drinks

Coffee Review **www.coffeereview.com**

Dark roast, decaf and just about every other bean and blend, delivered around the world in special sealed packs. Also includes tasting notes for the different blends.

Natashas Cafe **www.natashascafe.com**

Turkish coffee and all you need to make it – wonderful eclectic site that's good enough to ship around the world.

Roast and Post **www.realcoffee.co.uk**

Coffee facts and figures and the chance to buy a bag.

Shock **www.shockalots.com**

Eyelids drooping? Drink this hyper-caffeinated coffee that's 50% stronger than others – or visit the site that's a riot of yellow and red.

Whittard of Chelsea **www.whittard.com**
Dozens of speciality teas and Arabica coffees. There's also all the gear you'll need to make the tea or coffee and helpful hints.

Smokes

BC Specialties **www.bcspecialties.com**
Good source of cigar-related products from humidors and cutters to cases and lighters. Based in LA, they ship around the world.

Bonfiglioli Pipemaking **www.affari.com/bonfiglioli/**
The redoubtable Alberto makes some of the finest (and priciest) pipes in Italy.

Cigar Exports **www.cigarexport.com**
Impressive range of the best Cuban cigars plus top smokes from the Dominican Republic. Ships around the world – and they'll even ship these embargoed goods into the US. If it's confiscated by customs, they'll ship again for free!

CigsOnline **www.cigsonline.com**
Factory outlet in Virginia peddling cut-price American brands – but the shipping will knock out most of the savings.

Corona Cigar Company **www.coronacigar.com**
Good range of (non-native Cuban) cigars, plus accessories to store them in, cut them and smoke them.

James Barber Tobacconist **www.smoke.co.uk**
Age-old tobacconist selling a good range of pipes, tobacco, cigars and accessories from its base in West Yorkshire.

JJ Fox & Robert Lewis **www.jjfox.co.uk**
Just about the oldest cigar merchant with a great range of cigars, humidors and accessories. The order form's not secure so it's probably best to phone or visit the tiny shop in Mayfair.

Lighters Galore Plus **www.pipeshop.com**
Despite the name, the shop's piled high with pipes, cigars, humidors, knives and, of course, lighters.

Rizla+ **www.rizla.com**
Rolling paper trivia, games and late-night silliness for folk that roll their own. But the only thing you can buy online is branded clothing.

Smoker's Depot **www.cigars4u.com**
Fine selection of everything for the cigar smoker.

The Pipe Shop **www.thepipeshop.co.uk**
Tiny smoker's paradise sells pipes, cigars, tobacco and accessories from its base in Edinburgh – but online sales are rather primitive, and are only conducted via email.

The Tobacconist **www.the-tobacconist.co.uk**
Small shop, but a big range of cigars that they will ship to gasping surfers around the world.

//EDUCATIONAL

The Internet was developed by academics and in its early years was purely educational. Because of this, the majority of online educational material is free. The sister book, **The Virgin Family Internet Guide**, covers education, homework and teaching in great detail.

If you are looking for any type of educational material or information, the best place to start is the quite stunning BBC Education website at **www.bbc.co.uk/education/**. It's free – technically, it's paid for by British TV licence holders – but offers a vast range of guides, news, features and advice for any student, parent or teacher.

Of the commercial sites, some offer free teaching material (use the BBC Education site directory). Other sites mimic a real-life school and provide intensive additional tutoring for children who might need a little extra help with a subject. In return for a fee, you'll get a real tutor who'll help with questions via online chat.

Anglia Campus **www.angliacampus.com**
A new amalgam of the old BT CampusWorld and Anglia Interactive sites that charges a subscription, but it has plenty of resources and lessons for home and school study on the national curriculum.

Berlitz **www.berlitz.com**
Language teaching material, CDs, dictionaries and the famous phrase books.

BookSwap UK **http://208.245.63.64/bookswap/**
Swap old textbooks with other students.

Linguaphone **www.linguaphone.co.uk**
Buy any of their vast range of well-known language courses online.

Linkword **www.linkword.co.uk**
Learn a language in double-quick time with this special system.

Proops **www.proops.com**
Science kits that educate and are fun – solar power, mechanism, science, motors and so on.

Talkfast International **www.talkfast.com**
Modest range of software, dictionaries and tests to help learn a European language.

Teacher Smith **www.teachersmith.com**
Posters for classrooms and teaching.

The Educational Software Company **www.educational.co.uk**
Over 1,000 of the top educational software products at reasonable prices. There are decent descriptions for most entries and recom-

mendations help you pick the right program for your child's age and level.

The Virtual School **www.virtualschool.co.uk**

Quick, swot up on any GCSE or A-level subject online. For around £60 you'll get five weeks of tuition by email or chat session.

For much more about education, see The Virgin Family Internet Guide.

//ELECTRICAL GOODS

Cut-throat price wars are the rule in this business, with each supplier offering deep discounts and wide ranges. The nicer sites include good descriptions and photographs – the others expect you to use your imagination in the old-style pile-'em-high philosophy and, if they weren't so cheap, no one would visit. You'll find consumer electricals (hi-fi, TVs, videos, phones, cameras) mixed up in the same bag as household electricals (washing machines, dishwashers, vacuum cleaners, kettles). Whatever you want for your home, it's for sale in one of these shops and at a rock-bottom price.

21store.com **www.21store.com**

The latest digital gizmos – from PDAs to camcorders, GPS to mobiles – are lovingly described and sold from this site.

Audio Vision **www.shoppersuniverse.com**

Good range of home entertainment systems at decent prices – it's in the Shoppers Universe mall, so is easy to navigate. The mall also sells kitchen and domestic appliances in the Essential Electrics section and photographic equipment in the Photo Forum section.

BeDirect **www.bedirect.co.uk**

Toasters and tellies for sale, but no winner in the design stakes.

Box Clever **www.box-clever.com**
Stacks of home entertainment and domestic equipment for sale from retail chain Granada.

Dixons **www.dixons.co.uk**
Good range of home electronics, from TVs, videos and hi-fi equipment to cameras and computers.

DVDWorld **www.dvdworld.co.uk**
Very impressive site that's piled high with the kit you need to play the titles (which they also stock). Includes reviews, previews and news to keep you up to date with the latest.

Empire Direct **www.empiredirect.co.uk**
Save up to one third off high-street prices.

freeNET **http://freenet.estreet.co.uk**
Electrical and gas appliances (that's everything from fridges, cookers and hobs to hi-fis and camcorders). It's a hideous, garish design – but stick with it for the 25% discount you'll get off high-street prices.

Home Electrical Direct **www.hed.co.uk**
Good range of cut-price TVs, fridges and washing machines.

Innovations **www.innovations.co.uk**
Gadgets and wonderful inventions, some of them extremely silly.

Richer Sounds **www.richersounds.com**
Cut-price hi-fis piled floor-to-ceiling.

Shopping on the net **www.shoppingonthenet.co.uk**
Catch-all title, but really it's a general store with a reasonable range of household goods.

Quality Electrical Direct **www.qed-uk.com**
Very wide range of home electrical equipment, but the prices could be lower.

Unbeatable **www.unbeatable.co.uk**
Tons of home entertainment equipment – camcorders, cameras, TVs, videos and hi-fi systems at very keen prices.

We Sell It **www.we-sell-it.co.uk**
Modest range of brand name electrical appliances for sale: no fanfares, few descriptions and reasonable prices.

Woodalls **www.woodalls.co.uk**
Top electrical brand names, often at the lowest prices.

//FILMS

Buy the latest video at a discount price, watch classics on your browser or order up European art films for long, sleepless nights. Almost all the shopping sites sell films on videotapes and the new DVD format. Don't be tempted by the US prices – they use a different system and US videos won't work in the UK. Besides, there's more than enough here. Some of the largest retailers, such as WH Smith, have developed slick sites that combine books, music and video sales, but you'll get the best range, reviews and news from dedicated sites like Blackstar. If you want to find out more about a film, producer or star, visit the massive, and free, Internet Movie Database (**www.imdb.com**).

101cd.com **www.101cd.com**
A half-million catalogue list that carries videos and DVDs (plus books and games) from the UK and imports. Add your own review to any entry or pre-order forthcoming releases.

Blackstar **www.blackstar.co.uk**
Probably the best and certainly the biggest place to buy videos and DVDs in the UK. Vast range, discount prices and free delivery together with reviews, news and plenty of special offers. Plenty of nice touches, like the hyperlinked cast list – and these are cross-referenced to help you find all the films with that star.

DVDnet **www.dvdnet.co.uk**
Very strong on news and reviews, with a good selection of well-priced DVDs backed up with complete info and good descriptions about each film. You can also get the hardware to play it on.

DVDplus **www.dvdplus.co.uk**
Impressive presentation and design, with plenty of reviews and news. The titles are reasonably priced.

DVDstreet **www.dvdstreet.infront.co.uk**
Impressive store selling DVDs only. Very easy to navigate, great biogs and links, lots of news and reviews – free delivery and discounts make this a fab site.

DVDWorld **www.dvdworld.co.uk**
Great selection, very good prices, decent descriptions and reviews. Not as slick a design as DVDplus, but cheaper.

Entertainment Express **www.entexpress.com**
Good range of software, music CDs and videos – not the cheapest prices but decent write-ups and free delivery worldwide.

Eurocinema **www.eurocinema.com**
Virtual cinema that specialises in screening European films. There's an entrance ticket price but it's lower than a video rental.

Fat Sam's **www.fatsam.co.uk**
Friendly Sam sells over 200,000 books, tapes, CDs and videos. It's a clear site but hard to browse – you'll need to turn to the search engine all the time. Reasonable, but not the lowest, prices.

Film World **www.filmworld.co.uk**
Great site for movie buffs with an excellent range of independent, world and art films on video and DVD. Very good search engine and low prices. They've cleverly integrated clips from film.com (**www.film.com**) and listings from Scoot (**www.scoot.co.uk**).

Games and Videos **www.gamesandvideos.com**
Very good selection of videos and games for all platforms – search for the latest releases or foreign language titles. Not as chummy or friendly as Blackstar or Filmworld but does include mini synopses of major films.

HMV **www.hmv.co.uk**
Good prices, news and reviews of video and music CDs from the high-street giant.

The Interactive Music and Video Shop **www.imvs.com**
Very good range of music CDs and videos at excellent prices, and with brief write-ups.

VCI **www.vci.co.uk**
Particularly good on TV shows on video but with only a modest selection of films.

Video Paradise **www.videoparadise.com**
Good range, reasonable design – discounted 20% books, videos and games via WH Smith. The synopses and biogs aren't as good as Blackstar but you can keep up to date thanks to the onsite cyber-clerk, Brad, who will send you an email when similar titles are released.

VideoZone **www.videozone.co.uk**
A straightforward database of over 24,000 titles. No product reviews, descriptions or anything! But reasonable prices.

//FLOWERS AND GREETINGS

Sending flowers over the Internet is a strange notion but has proved so efficient and popular that it's one of the more unlikely success stories of the web. The biggest sites span the world and provide same- or next-day delivery in any country using local florists. Smaller local or national florists can provide cheaper or better service (and a wider choice of flowers) and can send flowers via courier for emergencies or forgotten anniversaries. When you visit an online flower shop, you'll see a whole range of bouquets pictured. You can choose one of the ready-made styles or create your own from seasonal flowers. Add a message, pay by credit card and your order is processed and delivered.

1-800 Flowers **www.1800flowers.com**
Probably the best site for flowers on the net – the leader in design and shopping experience. Great for overseas deliveries but anything back to the UK costs a bomb.

Bunches **www.bunches.co.uk**
Cheer someone up for under £15 – send a simple bunch of flowers anywhere in the UK. Alternatively, splash out for chocs, a teddy or a bigger bunch.

Clare Florist **www.clareflorist.co.uk**
Good range of hand-tied bouquets, arrangements and baskets of flowers.

Expressions Flowers and Balloons **www.expressions.co.uk**
Fresh, silk or dried flower arrangements, plus the inevitable balloons and teddies – delivered around the UK.

Flowers by Design **www.flowersbydesign.co.uk**
Custom bouquets and flower arrangements designed in-house then couriered to your door.

Flowers Direct **www.flowersdirectuk.co.uk**
Very good selection of flowers and flower arrangements that'll be sent by courier for next-day delivery in the UK. Tell them your important dates and you'll get an email to remind you.

GiftStore UK **www.giftstore.co.uk**
Not just chocs, flowers and cards – also games, books, videos, jewellery and toys. They can wrap and post anything to anywhere.

Interflora **www.interflora.co.uk**
Shop for flowers, bouquets and baskets, then send them within the UK or around the world.

Teleflorist **www.teleflorist.co.uk**
Interflora's big rival similarly works through independent florists (over 55,000 around the world). You can order bouquets, arrangements and even hampers, which are then delivered from the nearest local shop.

Supermarkets

The main UK supermarkets let you buy flowers and send them as a gift. Check out these sites:

Sainsbury's **www.sainsburys.co.uk**
You need to register as a member first (that means visiting a store).

Tesco **www.tesco.co.uk**
Uses Interflora.

Somerfield **www.somerfield.co.uk**
Modest range of five bouquets from this strangely sombre store.

//FOOD

Web fanatics must have vast appetites judging by the number of food and foodie sites online. There are shops offering speciality bread, foie gras, organic meat and fresh fish. It's a great way of finding small, local producers selling highly original food. You'll find the web is great when shopping for exotic gourmet ingredients, but it's also just as good for everyday groceries with a full weekly shop at Tesco or Sainsbury's online – leaving the in-store picker to deal with the Saturday crush, then deliver to your home.

One of the oddities of this food section is that it shows up regional differences in getting online. There are hundreds of sites selling

Scottish foods, more sites offering American food, but nothing from Wales or Ireland. Looking for speciality foods from other countries can be a problem in both language and import restrictions. When searching, you'll probably need to enter key words in English and the local language (or use the country-specific versions of Excite! and Yahoo!). For example, trying to find authentic Italian pasta produced just one hit – an importer in the US who in turn would not export.

Although this section just covers food, don't forget to look at the other relevant sections in this guide for coffee, wine, beer & sweets.

Bakoven **http://home.clara.net/cvp39/bakoven/table1.html**
Traditional bakers specialising in organic German-style bread – how it's made, why it's great and, if you're tempted, they'll deliver anywhere in the UK.

BritsAbroad **www.britsabroad.co.uk**
Stock up on vital supplies of Marmite and HP sauce, shipped to wherever you might find yourself.

Caledonian Curry **www.caledoniancurry.co.uk**
Splendid eccentric site from chef Ian Smith – cooks fine curries (ready to microwave) with Scottish venison, rabbit and other local ingredients. At the moment it's mail order only, but roll on the secure shopping site!

Cheese **www.cheese.com**
Simple cheddar, yes, but also over 500 other cheeses listed and arranged by name, taste and texture and country. A similarly extensive and obsessive (if not quite so polished) site is CheeseNet (www.wgx.com/cheesenet/).

Chinese Recipe Collections **www.nauticom.net/www/emlu/ch/recipe.htm**
Fine collection of links that point you towards dedicated sites on

almost every aspect of Chinese cooking, recipes and ingredients.

Curry House **www.curryhouse.co.uk**
Everything about curry – where to eat it, how to make it and, thanks to mail-order supplier Chilli Willie, you can get the spices online.

Earth Foods **www.earthfoods.co.uk**
Where to buy your organic peanut butter and chocolate.

Epicurious Food **http://food.epicurious.com**
The message is, 'If you eat, visit this site' – and it's not wrong. Vast site that shows just how much can be written about food, recipes and drink. It's US-centric but, with this amount of information, who cares?

Global Gourmet **www.globalgourmet.com**
A good all-rounder for gourmets and gourmands – not quite up to Epicurious, but easy to manage.

Gourmet World **www.gourmet-world.co.uk**
Essentials of life – foie gras, truffle oil and wine supplied here – but they aren't well described.

Groceries **www.groceries.org.uk**
Where to find the cheapest supplies of groceries.

Heinz **www.heinz-direct.co.uk**
Snap up a crate of ketchup, baby food or beans.

Kitchenlink **www.kitchenlink.com**
Great starting place, stacked high with links to almost every worthwhile culinary site on the web.

Le Gourmet Français on-line **www.jayfruit.com**
Fresh truffles, foie gras, even organic food delivered.

Macdonalds Smoked Produce **www.smokedproduce.co.uk**
If it can be smoked, they'll do it. Cheeses, trout, venison, duck, pigeon, kangaroo, ostrich and, naturally, haggis.

Morel Bros., Cobbett & Son **www.morel.co.uk**
Wonderful site for the gourmet – impressive range of 350 foods, each with masses of detail.

Organics Direct **www.organicsdirect.com**
Don't panic, it's organic. Food, chocolates, even cotton socks are delivered anywhere in the UK.

Real Meat Company **www.realmeat.co.uk**
Caring farmers selling meat produced without chemicals.

Sainsbury's **www.sainsburys.co.uk**
Cumbersome way to do your weekly shop. First, visit your local store with a bar-code gun and build up your own basic shopping list. Now you can order from the website – but it can be painfully slow and one gets the feeling it would be more reliable to phone.

Salami.com **www.salami.com**
Good, honest New York Italian salami, sausage, cheese, pasta and sauces – Vinnie will ship them around the world, or send someone a virtual sausage card.

Scottish Store **www.scottish-store.co.uk**
Reasonable range of typical Scottish foods for sale – cheese, smoked salmon, oysters, even mussels. Very few pix, and descriptions are short.

Teddington Cheese **www.teddingtoncheese.co.uk**
Bright, clear presentation shows off fabulous cheeses from a tiny shop run by very knowledgeable obsessives.

The Organic Delivery Company **www.organicdelivery.co.uk**
Organic veg, fruit and wines delivered weekly around London.

The Village Bakery **www.village-bakery.co.uk**
Biscuits, breads, buns and cakes – all organic and from a wood-fired oven in a charming stone bakery in deepest Cumbria.

Tesco **www.tesco.co.uk**
Choose your items from the virtual aisles – no need to visit a shop with a barcode scanner. And you can even get a free Internet account.

Thorntons **www.thorntons.co.uk**
Toffee, fudge, chocs, hampers and the occasional mug.

Shetland Smokehouse **www.shetlandseafood.co.uk**
Fished from the southern end of Shetland, you can buy the salmon, haddock, herring, cod and mackerel direct from the enthusiastic, if rather basic, site. There's no secure ordering, but they'll call you back for your credit card details.

Waitrose **www.waitrose.com**
Not everything from the supermarket, just organic food and wine.

Wessex Provender **http://provender.net**
Friendly West Country charm helps keep this site ticking – loads of cheeses, meats and organic veg, plus recipes.

Wild Alaska Smoked Salmon **www.smoked-fish.com**
Coho, sockeye or Pacific salmon, caught in and shipped from Alaska – straight to your table.

//GAMBLING

If you're mad, rich or both, you could try your luck with the online gambling sites set up to take your money and, occasionally, pay out. If you follow the form then bet online – on horse races, the dogs or any other event. For the truly brave, you can visit a casino and try blackjack or poker. You pay your stakes in all the gambling sites using a debit or credit card. The online bookies repay you via your card's account, whereas the casinos generally send you a draft through the post (often in Swiss francs).

Blue Square **www.bluesq.com**
Sports news, results and a cool, smart betting service.

Casinos of the South Pacific **www.ck.cosp.com**
Poker and the other games deep in the South Pacific. Payment's in Swiss francs.

Centrebet Sports Betting **www.centrebet.com.au**
Based in Alice Springs, try betting on any event in Australia or around the world – they pay directly to your account.

InterLOTTO **www.interlotto.li**
Based in Liechtenstein, it operates a range of different weekly lotteries paying out millions. Part of the proceeds go to the Red Cross, and it's audited by Coopers & Lybrand.

Island Casino **www.islandcasino.com**
Full casino (blackjack, baccarat, poker) here on the mysterious, unnamed island – or you can bet on sports events around the world.

Sportingbet.com **www.sportingbet.com**
Slick site that lets you place bets on almost any sporting event. Based in Alderney, it's also tax-free!

Sporting Life **www.sporting-life.com**
Who'll win what, when and why.

UK Betting **www.ukbetting.com**
Not as flash as the Sportingbet site but quicker and easier to use. Unfortunately, you'll be taxed as with a normal bookie.

//GAMES AND HOBBIES

Trains, model planes or radio-controlled cars – whatever your pastime or hobby there are specialist shops online. There are probably more radio-controlled car shops than any other, closely followed by kites – an unexpected find – but both are great fun. If you're shopping for traditional games, you'll find it's easier to play an online version than find a real edition to buy for home. There are dozens of stamp-collector's sites, but they don't show pictures and use jargon that excludes beginners or young collectors. And while adult train enthusiasts can buy handmade brass locos for thousands, if you want a cheap first train set try the toys section of this directory.

Hobbies

3rd Rail Models **www.3rdrail.com**
Small selection of high-quality brass model trains – expensive but stunning models for big boys.

Big Little Railroad Shop **www.biglittle.com**
Track to train sets, locos to stations, there's everything for train enthusiasts here.

BoLINK R/C Cars **www.bolink.com**
Radio-controlled cars, kits and bodies – direct from Georgia, USA.

BRP Racing Products **www.brpracing.com**
Set up your own racing team with this collection of radio-controlled cars, bodies, tyres and accessories.

Caboose **www.thecaboose.com**
Over 2,800 brass model trains for the rich and obsessive train enthusiast.

Crown Agents Stamp Bureau **www.casb.co.uk**
Buy the latest UK stamps from the makers – the Crown.

Dave's Wonderful World of Yo-Yos **www.nmia.com/~whistler/yo-yos.html**
Yo-yo heaven. Vintage yo-yos for sale.

Hobby Lobby International **www.hobby-lobby.com**
Radio-controlled boats, planes and helicopters at low prices from the US.

Portsmouth Stamp Shop **www.portsmouthstamps.co.uk**
Good search facility and thousands of stamps from around the world. Modest descriptions – also sells cigarette cards.

Robin Hood Stamp Company **www.robinhood-stamp.co.uk**
Friendly site packed with stamps from around the world. Modest descriptions and no pix.

Stanley Gibbons **www.stangib.com**
Gets licked by the competition – rather uninspiring site and a very basic ordering system.

Toolpost **www.toolpost.co.uk**
Switch off the lathe and head over to a site packed with products for woodturners and woodworkers.

Tower Hobbies **www.towerhobbies.com**
Your first place to call for anything to do with radio-controlled models – thousands of items listed and shipped around the world.

Games

The Kite Shop **www.kiteshop.co.uk**
Bag yourself an aerobic four-line traction kite – or a simple triangle with a bit of string. Great site for beginners and advanced kite enthusiasts.

The Kite Store **www.kitestore.com/kite/**
Kites and yo-yos for kids and bird fans from the US.

The London Chess Centre **www.chess.co.uk**
Collection of books, videos, links to clubs and news on local tournaments. Save precious playing time and subscribe to their email e-zine.

World of Games **www.worldofgames.com**
Dinner's over – time for a little murder-mystery adventure. Buy the kit here.

//GARDENING

You can actually order a whole new garden over the web. Suppliers of sheds, stone pots, spades and compost all have shops waiting for your order. However, most gardeners will want to shop for things that grow. The biggest sites are in the US, but the strict customs regulations make it impossible to buy anything except seeds. For young plants, bulbs, shrubs, trees or roses, you'll find UK-based garden centres and specialist suppliers provide speedy delivery to stock up your borders.Some sites, such as Crocus (**www.crocus.co.uk**) will even help design your borders then come out and help plant out your flowers and shrubs.

Architectural Heritage **www.architectural-heritage.co.uk**
Antique iron garden furniture to add style to your patio or gazebo.

Birstall Garden Centre **www.birstall.co.uk**
Very impressive garden centre selling everything from sheds to stone slabs, seeds to roses.

British Gardening Online **www.oxalis.co.uk**
Friendly garden centre selling seeds, equipment and plants, plus plenty of information about gardens and garden centres open around the UK. Not as complete or slick as the US sites but improving, and much cheaper on shipping!

eSeeds.com **www.eseeds.com**
Excellent selection of unusual seeds, bulbs and garden tools shipped out from Canada (there are also plants, but it's totally impractical to post these around the world).

Exhibition Seeds **www.exhibition-seeds.co.uk**
Fantastic range of vegetable, grass and herb seeds.

Garden Centre **www.gardenworld.co.uk**
Find your local suppliers and garden centres in this directory, plus news of events and a few Q&A features.

Gardening Club **www.gardening-club.co.uk**
Very useful advice to help keep your garden blooming. But needs more in it and more for sale.

GardeningStore **www.gardeningstore.com**
Official shop from the Royal Horticultural Society, with a good range of books and very few plants.

Garden.com **www.garden.com**
Vast, wonderful garden centre with masses of advice, online planning and over 15,000 products – you should be able to place international orders by the time you read this.

Garden Shop **www.thegardenshop.co.uk**
Swish garden furniture.

Harkness Roses **www.roses.co.uk**
Select specimens from this specialist dealer and news from the prickly world of rose growing.

Seed Potatoes International **www.seed-potatoes-international.co.uk**
Exactly what it says it is. Spuds worldwide.

Shrubs Direct **www.shrubsdirect.com**
Boost your borders with a little something ordered from a range of nearly 1,000 shrubs from Cheshire.

Tyler's **www.tylers.co.uk**
Good selection of plants, fences, benches and stones – you can view the catalogue and prices online, but you'll have to phone to order.

UK Gardening Tools **www.pelcogarden.com**
Gloves, weeders and a modest range of other essentials.

West Lindsey Growers Ltd **www.wlg-ltd.com**
Thousands of baby plants available online – but the payment system isn't secure, so best to phone.

//GIFTS AND CARDS

These sites get busy at Christmas. Find the perfect present, from a sleek steel executive gizmo to a delicate porcelain doll. And if you'd rather just say hello, without the expense or formality of a present, send an electronic card (by email) – choose from the specialist shops or even create your own customised card.

800 Hampers **www.800Hampers.com**
Hampers packed with goodies from Scotland.

American Greetings **www.americangreetings.com**
Choose a card, write a message and leave it to AG to send it around the world. Or choose one of the free email cards.

Archie McPhee **www.mcphee.com**
Oddball toys and gifts. Bendy men, children's cat alarm clocks, sumo wrestler fans for hot summer days.

Clearwater Hampers **www.hamper.com**
Wonderful, tempting wicker hampers for every occasion and event – or, if you prefer, there's wine, chocs and corporate gifts – delivered from the UK base around the world.

CRC Greetings Direct **www.greetingsdirect.co.uk**
Nice cards from a good cause – Cancer Research Campaign – that can be personalised. You'll have to post them yourself, though.

Cybercard **www.cybercard.co.uk**
Choose one of the designs, what to say inside and pay up £2.50 and the site will print it out with your message and send it off.

Daisychain **www.daisychain.co.uk**
'Ever so adorable' porcelain figures and dolls, china animals and cherubs.

Eastern Origins **www.easternorigins.com**
You know they'll just love that wooden Buddha or that carved elephant.

Elite Scribe **www.elitescribe.com**
For the writer in your life. A real ink pen from a good selection of the smartest names.

Fortnum & Mason **www.fortnumandmason.com**
Hampers, wines, chocs and gifts delivered direct.

Fridgedoor.com **www.fridgedoor.com**
You're gonna need a damn big fridge to use even a fraction of these fridge magnets. Terrific range from The Beatles to Bond, Austin Powers to South Park.

GiftStore UK **www.giftstore.co.uk**
Not just chocs, flowers and cards – also games, books, videos, jewellery and toys. They can wrap and post anything, anywhere. Masses of nice products and great cards.

Hallmark **www.hallmark.com**
Great range of cards and gifts that you can personalise and have sent – or choose from over 1,000 free email cards.

Hammacher Schlemmer **www.hammacher.com**
The big (and unpronounceable) name in eccentric gifts on the US mall scene – pick up an electric golf buggy, moisturizing rubber gloves (very scary) or a wind-defying umbrella. Staggering shipping costs abroad, but well worth a visit.

Innovations **www.innovations.co.uk**

From shiatsu massage kits to screwdrivers that grip; hundreds of gizmos that sound fantastically useful to someone.

Purple Pom Pom **http://purplepompom.co.uk**

Chic and contemporary things for sale – steel alarm clocks, jolly children's toys and gear, sleek executive toys, Dalmatian-print towels and much more besides.

Slow Dazzle **www.slowdazzle.com**

Keep track of time with an interesting range of calendars.

The Aardmarket **http://aardmarket.aardman.com**

Nice site, Grommit – pass the Wensleydale. Here's home to Wallace and chums as models, toys, rucksacks and pictures.

//HEALTH AND FITNESS

In the US, sites dedicated to medicines (such as the vast drugstore.com) are taking over from local pharmacies, but in the UK there's resistance to this change. In the UK and most other countries, pharmacies won't supply drugs or complete prescriptions over the web; at the time of writing, Britain's biggest high street chemist, Boots, has a rather feeble informational site, but sells nothing. Taking the US as a role model, this situation is sure to change. The dynamic drugstore.com now has links to many local drug stores in the US – go online to order your prescription and pick it up from the traditional store. However, most US sites won't ship medicine outside their country due to the different international regulations. With natural and homeopathic remedies, there's no such barrier – shops supplying aromatherapy oils, herb-based concoctions and Chinese medicines will ship anywhere.

Appledore **www.appledore.co.uk**

Find a new toothbrush. Dental products and advice.

Condomania **www.condoms4u.com**
Cartoons lead you to cut-price brand names. Or, for a similar choice in a more sombre, serious setting, try Condom (www.condom.co.uk).

Contact Lens Solutions **www.contact-lens.co.uk**
The site's name is a give-away. Cut price stuff for the shortsighted.

Culpeper **www.culpeper.co.uk**
Herbs and herb-based products for cooking, cleaning, beauty, aromatherapy, healing and health.

drugstore.com **www.drugstore.com**
Virtual pharmacist provides almost every medical and health product you can imagine. Medical, beauty and nutritional information – you can even buy direct from the US.

First Aid Direct **www.firstaid-direct.co.uk**
First aid kits for the home.

Fleur Aromatherapy **www.fleur.co.uk**
Oils and kits for smelly massages – and a very pleasurable experience.

Freeman's Homeopathic Pharmacy **www.freechem.co.uk**
Homeopathic remedies and preparations, information and online ordering.

G.Baldwin & Co **www.baldwins.co.uk**
Vast range of over 3,000 herbs, aromatherapy treatments, supplements, health foods and cosmetics.

Garden Pharmacy **www.garden.co.uk**
Herbal and homeopathic remedies.

LA Muscle **www.lamuscle.com**
Turn flab to muscle with lots of nutritional products, advice and tips. With product names like 'sculpt' and 'fat stripper', you know what to expect.

Optilabs **www.optilabs.com**
Spectacle lens manufacturers who will fit lenses to any frames – much cheaper than the high street.

Tea Tree Oil **www.teatree.co.uk**
Captain Cook named it, now you can find out about it and buy it – particularly good for skin conditions.

The Health Shop **www.thehealthshop.co.uk**
Good value vitamins, minerals and supplements.

Vision Express **www.visionexpress.co.uk**
Buy sunglasses and contacts online from the chain store.

Vitamin Shoppe **www.vitaminshoppe.com**
Stock up on ginkgo or get bulk supplies of vitamin C from the US megastore. Massive range of vitamins and supplements shipped around the world.

//HOME

You can shop on the Internet for rugs, paints, wallpapers and all kinds of things for the house. You can even get advice on colour schemes and DIY tips. Even furniture's easy to buy – but the UK suppliers are not quite up to the quality of their US counterparts – who, unsurprisingly, prefer not to ship sofas across the Atlantic.

All-Clad Online **www.metrokitchen.com**
Bright shiny pots and pans – from top maker All-Clad.

Architectural Heritage **www.architectural-heritage.co.uk**
Antique-panelled rooms and iron garden furniture.

Bean Bag Planet **www.beanbagplanet.com**
More beanbags than you could ever flop into – for kids, adults and spineless dudes. For a vast bag, the size of small bed, try Bean Bag City (www.beanbag.com).

Chadder and Co. **www.chadder.com**
Antique bathtubs, taps and shower fittings.

Chef's Store **www.chefs-store.com**
Everything the home or pro chef might ever need in the kitchen – supplied at discount prices. Also includes some specialist foods.

Cooksons Tools **www.cooksons.com**
Over 27,000 hand and power tools for the DIY obsessed.

Cooks Kitchen **www.kitchenware.co.uk**
Kettles, chopping boards and all sorts of other cooking things.

Country Desks **www.countrydesks.co.uk**
A traditional English furniture shop based in Berkhampstead now selling over the web. Good range of traditional country desks, computer desks, chairs, bookcases, filing cabinets and lamps. Clear pictures and detailed descriptions.

Craft & Design London **http://craftdesign-london.com**
Trendy and expensive ceramics, furniture, glassware and metalwork from the latest young designers.

Edwards China **www.edwardschina.co.uk**
Wedgwood, Minton, Denby and Dalton – porcelain tableware or gifts at prices to beat the high street, painstakingly cushion-wrapped and delivered from Staffordshire.

Feng Shui **www.feng-shui-shop.co.uk**
Create the perfect balance with the help of these accessories.

Flames **http://flames.estreet.co.uk**
Fireplaces online. Lots of helpful info to help you choose the best fit.

Futon Direct **www.futondirect.co.uk**
Sleep close to the floor with futon frames and pads. You can also try Futons Direct (www.futons-direct.co.uk) or Mariko San (www.redworth.co.uk/mariko-san/).

Home Creations **www.myinternet.co.uk/home/**
Hundreds of kitchen appliances from over 30 brands sold at low prices.

Home Zone **www.shoppersuniverse.com**
Furniture, bedding, and accessories for the showroom home.

Internet Wallpaper Store **www.wallpaperstore.com**
Steam off the regency stripe and choose one of the 14,000 wallpapers, borders or fabrics here – with international shipping.

Iron Bed Company **www.ironbed.co.uk**
As you might have guessed, they sell iron beds. Plus bedlinen, mattresses and pillows to fit.

Marc Newson Design **www.marc-newson.com**
Trend-setting furniture and objects from this London-based specialist.

McCord **www.mccord.uk.com**
Simple, fashionable home and garden furniture and accessories – few details and fuzzy pictures are a let-down.

Nottingham Lace Market **www.nottingham-lace.co.uk**
Pretty lace tablecloths, hankies, screens and purses; like the products, the site is rather fussy but the quality's good.

Rabid Home **www.rabidhome.com**
Stylish, quirky accessories, like mugs, letter-openers, pens, pads and other lifestyle stuff. Just perfect for your loft-style apartment.

Replacements Ltd **www.replacements.com**
Crash! Now you've only got five dinner plates from your precious collection. Try this company in the US – they have over 100,000 patterns of plates, glass and china.

Screwfix **www.screwfix.com**
Not just screws but a huge range of tools, doors, bolts, blades and kits.

Space 2 **www.space2.com**
Arrange your study: furniture built to house your computer.

Straad Direct **www.straad.co.uk**
Stylish furniture, beds, sofas and giant lava lamps.

Thistle Joinery **www.thistlejoinery.co.uk**
Let a team of craftsmen design your bookcases, libraries, studies, home offices or wardrobes.

//INSURANCE

Insurance quotes are now calculated using databases to compare crime ratings for different postcodes, ages and professions. As a result, it's a perfect industry to transfer to the web, cutting out the human phone operator and giving consumers direct access to the quoting software – online. Many of the leading insurance companies can provide instant quotes, even instant coverage for your home, car or pet. The individual insurers often include online forms on their sites to let you ask for a personalised quote. However, to find the cheapest quote on the market, use one of the specialist general sites – such as ScreenTrade, Car Quote or Home Quote.

AA **www.theaa.co.uk**
Get insurance here (car, home, travel or breakdown).

Admiral **www.admiral-insurance.co.uk**
Ask for a quote for car insurance online, but you're likely to get the answer by phone or post.

Car Quote **www.carquote.co.uk**
Fill in the online forms and you'll get car insurance quotes emailed or posted to you from a range of suppliers.

Eagle Star Insurance **www.eaglestardirect.co.uk**
Ask for a quote, then buy the insurance – online.

Home Quote UK **http://home.quote.co.uk**
Fill in your details and you'll get house insurance quotes from half a dozen companies.

RAC **www.rac.co.uk**
Sort out your car insurance (plus a mass of travel information and resources for anyone with a car).

Screen Trade **www.screentrade.co.uk**
Reduce your insurance by comparing umpteen different suppliers – for car, house and travel.

Under the Sun **www.underthesun.co.uk**
Online travel insurance quotes.

Woolwich Insurance **www.woolwich.co.uk**
Online quotes for home insurance. For pet insurance, they'll call you back.

//JEWELLERY AND WATCHES

It's hard to try on and admire the jewellery or watches that you'll find for sale in specialist stores on the web – no one's cottoned on to the virtual mannequin idea used by some clothes shops (like **www.landsend.com**). But it would help. Instead, you get discount prices on antique and modern jewellery and watches. Before you buy, make sure that you get a certificate of authenticity – to prove the gold is gold and that the watch hasn't come straight from someone else's wrist. If you place an order, opt for the insured recorded delivery or courier dispatch option – or your new gems could get lost in the post. You'll also find masses of both jewellery and watches sold in the online auctions – particularly eBay (**www.ebay.com**) – but see the chapter on auctions for tips on buying safely at these sites.

Clocks and watches

City Clocks **www.cityclocks.co.uk**
A century of experience in repairing, selling and building clocks, barometers and watches.

Swatch Heaven **www.topbrands.net**
Every conceivable Swatch is here.

WatchFactory.com **www.watchfactory.com**
Brand name watches at the best prices – a clearing-house for over 100 models; low-cost shipping from the US.

Watchmart.com **www.watchmart.com**
Fill in a form with the details of the prestige watch you're after and the dealer with the cheapest price will contact you with the good news – expect to save up to 35% off brands like Ebel, Patek Phillippe, Cartier and Tag Heuer.

Jewellery

Fortunoff **www.fortunoff.com**
Load down the lady in your life with jewellery or watches from this established US store.

GemNet **www.gemnet.co.uk**
A good place to start shopping – a busy arcade of jewellers selling watches, diamonds, amber, modern and antique pieces, plus information, guarantees and help preventing thefts.

Gold Jewellery Online **www.gold-jewelry.co.uk**
Gold jewellery with a Scottish flavour – individual shops carry pieces inspired by Rennie Mackintosh and traditional clan or highland designs. Good design, but the pictures could do with a polish.

Great British Jewels **www.gbj.co.uk**
An odd mix of jewellery, paintings and sculptures from UK designers.

Half Price Jewellers **www.hpj.co.uk**
Low-cost jewellery from the high-street chain with the same name.

H Thomas Jewels **www.jewels.co.uk**
Stockport's net-friendly jeweller provides a modest selection of watches and rings.

Ice Cool **www.icecool.co.uk**
Classic or modern gold and diamond jewellery. Great photos show off the ice to good effect – and there's a 5% discount.

Jewellery Direct **www.jewellery-direct.com**
Good range of gold and silver jewellery for men and women with plenty of pictures to show you what to expect.

Robinson & Stirling **www.robinson-and-stirling.com**
Individual, handmade silver jewellery

//MOTORBIKES

If you want to buy a bike, visit one of the specialist dealers that cover a particular brand or type of bike. If you're looking for a second-hand ride, the big classified papers (*Exchange and Mart*, *Loot* and *Bike Trader*) all have thousands of ads that are fast and easy to search. You can search the database for a bike that fits your exact spec and is a convenient ride from home. Better still, set up an email alert to be sure you're the first to hear when an ad comes in for your perfect bike. Accessories, clothes and even spare parts are all listed and indexed on the bigger sites.

Beedspeed International **http://homepages.enterprise.net/beedspeed/**
Every grommet, spring and trim panel to mend your scooter.

BikeNet **www.bikenet.com**
Slick UK site with the latest bike tests, biker discussion groups, race reports and classifieds.

Bike Trader **www.biketrader.co.uk**
The biggest range of bikes for sale with a database of over 8,000 classified ads.Exchange and Mart (www.exchangeandmart.co.uk).

Board Silly **www.boardsilly.co.uk**
Look cool or silly (depending where you are) on a tiny motorised skateboard or an electric scooter.

Cambridge Lambretta Workshops **www.lambretta.co.uk**
Choose a new Italian scooter or buy spares to keep yours on the road.

Cannon Motorcycles **www.cannon-bmw.co.uk**
BMW dealer with lists of new and used bikes on offer – but you can advertise your own unwanted spares on its classified noticeboard.

Metal Horse **www.metalhorse.co.uk**
Experience a 'hog' in leafy Surrey – these specialists will rent or arrange a tour for you on a Harley Davidson.

Mettbikes **www.mettbikes.com**
Thousands of spares for hundreds of bikes – a fast search engine finds the part you're looking for.

Motorcycle City **www.motorcycle-city.co.uk**
Slick site with swish bikes and loads of accessories that can be ordered online.

NetBikes **www.netbikes.yks.com**
Classifieds for exotica – and a particular soft spot for Ducati and Triumph bikes.

Piaggio **www.piaggio.com**
The latest Vespas. One of the trendiest scooter brands on the market.

ScooterZone **www.scooterzone.co.uk**
Beat the traffic, buy a scooter.

//MUSEUM SHOPS

Forget the cultural experience of a museum and head straight for the shop. Most museums around the world now provide exhibitions on the web (from the Louvre – **http://mistral.culture.fr/louvre/louvrea.htm** – to the Tate – **www.tate.org.uk**), and many have set up their gift shops online. Buy posters and prints from your favourite museum and get it shipped home without the tiresome bother of actually visiting the exhibition.

Jerry Lewis Comedy Museum and Store **www.jerrylewiscomedy.com**
Stock up on laughs from the comedian's store – no shopping cart yet, but you can order by email.

Louvre **http://mistral.culture.fr/louvre/louvrea.htm**
French cultural icon also sells books, cards and posters.

Metropolitan Museum of Art Store **http://metmuseum.netcart.com**
Save the airfare, shop in New York's classy museum store for clothes, art and accessories.

Museum Company **www.museumcompany.com**
Art, jewellery and toys from museums around the world.

Museum of Modern Art Online Store **http://store.moma.org**
Super-stylish site and products from the most original shop (and museum) in the US.

MuseumShop@Home **www.museumshop.com**
Don't bother with the exhibits, just hit the shops – mostly smaller, local US museums.

Sea Treasures Museum Store **www.seatreasurestore.com**
Don't bother diving to the deep, you can buy pieces of eight, gold escudos and other stuff.

Tate Gallery **www.tate.org.uk**
Posters, cards and T-shirts from the best UK online art museum.

Tech Museum Store **http://store.thetech.org**
Techie and mind-twisting toys and games from the computer badlands of Silicon Valley.

//MUSIC

Music CDs, cassette tapes, DATs and even old-fashioned vinyl records have, with books, taken the biggest chunk of commerce on the web. There are dozens of vast sites with a catalogue of hundreds of thousands of CDs, often at very low prices. But, like any other area on the net, the small specialist site will probably have a better range for your particular beat – from jungle to ska. As with the book sites, use the ShopSmart (**www.shopsmart.com**) or Taxi (**www.mytaxi.co.uk**) sites to track down the cheapest place to buy your chart albums, but use the specialist shops for range, reviews and samples. MP3 files are set to take the world by storm – they provide a convenient way of storing CD-quality stereo music that can be played back on your computer or in a tiny portable player. New sites sell MP3 albums, but there are far more sites listing pirated files.

101cd.com **www.101cd.com**
Not just music CDs – the half-million catalogue list also carries books, DVDs, videos and games from the UK and imports. Add your

own review to any entry (rather like Amazon) or pre-order forthcoming releases.

Abbey Records **www.abbeyrecords.co.uk**
Good selection of second-hand records.

Action Records **www.action-records.co.uk**
Three unique points: one, they still sell vinyl; two, they also have a real shop; three, they also have their own music label. A great place to shop for indie and mainstream records.

All Star **www.allstarmag.com**
Music news and reviews from around the world; part of CD-NOW, so you can buy once you've read.

Audiostreet **www.audiostreet.com**
Read, listen and buy – from a choice of more than 100,000 CDs – an excellent site that includes track listings for the bestsellers, sample audio clips, news and charts.

Blackmail Music **www.blackmail.co.uk**
Packed with every type of music from ska to rockabilly, plus a special section just for Elvis Costello. Each entry includes track listings and the cover artwork.

BorrowORrob **www.borroworrob.com**
Charming name, fantastic choice. Over 500,000 titles, most at discount prices.

Boxman **www.boxman.co.uk**
Nice, clean site with CDs neatly organised by category – includes track titles but you might need to go over to All Music Guide (**www.allmusic.com**) to listen to samples.

CD Paradise **www.cdparadise.com**
Enormous stores of CDs, records and cassettes to browse through, with short factual descriptions and buyers' reviews to help recommend. Good prices and plenty of discounts from WH Smith.

CD Zone **www.cdzone.co.uk**
OK for quick searches, but try somewhere else (like Dotmusic) if you want a leisurely stroll to browse.

Cheap or What! **www.cow.co.uk**
Visit this workmanlike site for the great selection of CDs and videos at discount prices – with free delivery thrown in for good measure. If you want the top chart albums at the lowest prices, try Discount CDs (**www.discountcds.net**).

Dotmusic **www.dotmusic.com**
Pretty much the perfect mix of gossip, official news, previews, biogs and, to fund it all, sales of CDs.

Entertainment Express **www.entexpress.com**
Music, videos and computer games crammed into the one site.

Fat Sam's **www.fatsam.co.uk**
Over 200,000 CDs as well as books and videos. Easy to browse and tempts with plenty of offers.

Funkyworld Records **www.funkworld.co.uk**
Whip off your shades and check out the house, garage and hardcore vinyl on sale.

GEMM **www.gemm.com**
Track down hard-to-find CDs with a useful search tool that looks in all the new and second-hand online stores.

Heyday Mail Order **www.heyday-mo.com**
The best psychedelic music housed in surprisingly plain site.

HMV **www.hmv.co.uk**
High-street music store for mainstream soul, jazz, pop and classic CDs, DVDs and videos.

Littlestar **www.littlestar.co.uk**
A good range of CDs at competitive prices and, best of all, music

samples from new albums, reviews, descriptions and cover artwork – all wrapped in a very user-friendly shop.

Lycos **www.lycos.co.uk**
Search engine gets an honourable mention here because it's about the best place to search for bootleg (and occasionally legal) MP3 files to download and play.

Magpie Direct Music **www.magpiedirect.com**
Original albums from the original artists (no copies or re-issues) from the 40s to the 80s – great for collectors and the nostalgic.

Magpie Records **www.magpierecords.co.uk**
The latest indie, dance, rock and reggae that you'll never find on the high street.

MDC Classic Music **www.mdcmusic.co.uk**
Excellent selection of classical music.

Ministry of Sound **www.ministryofsound.co.uk**
Your name's on the guest list, step inside – to the tunes from the groovy London club.

Moving Music **www.movingmusic.co.uk**
Super-cheap CDs, tapes and videos – most for under a fiver.

MP3.com **www.mp3.com**
Plenty of news on copyright laws, the software you need to play back the files and a good range of new indie bands using MP3 to preview their sample tracks. Thousands of unknowns and a smattering of classical, but no major artists.

Music365 **www.music365.com**
Brilliant site packed with reviews, news, and chat about bands, albums and gigs. Read what's hot, then buy the ticket, CD, or video.

Music Capital **www.musiccapital.com**
Chart hits, plus plenty of special imports and dance tracks from Capital FM.

Organ1st **www.organ.co.uk**
Your own Hammond organ recordings to play again and again. Hundreds of jazz, theatre and classic organ music on CD.

ShopSmart **www.shopsmart.com**
Find the cheapest book, video or CD with the UK bargain finder's shopping tool (see Chapter 3 for more details).

Taxi **www.mytaxi.co.uk**
Find the cheapest book, video or CD with this neat tool to help find bargains in UK shops (see Chapter 3 for more details).

Past Perfect **www.pastperfect.com**
Sounds of the 20s (and 30s and 40s) lovingly remastered to remove the crackles and scratches.

Razorcuts **www.razorcuts.com**
Browse the site for tracks you want – from jazz to lounge, classic to disco – and create your own custom CD. Cool.

Rocktropolis **www.rocktropolis.com**
A souped-up music store with news, features and samples to tempt you to buy.

Timewarp Records **www.tunes.co.uk/timewarp**
Dig up an eclectic range of underground jazz, funk, soul and Latin music.

Uptown Records **www.uptownrecords.com**
If you can dance to it, it's here.

VCI **www.vci.co.uk**
Modest selection, but great descriptions and recommendations from the giant publisher and distributor of music, videos and books.

Vinyl Tap Records **www.vinyltap.co.uk**
Top stop for collectors with records, T-shirts, tour programmes and other memorabilia.

//MUSICAL INSTRUMENTS

Musicians will love the web. It's a great place to look for your next instrument – or sheet music – from either specialist suppliers or second-hand ads. Perhaps as a result of the popularity of the online record superstores selling CDs and MP3 files, there's a good selection of shops for musicians. The large instrument manufacturers, such as Fender (guitars) and Yamaha (keyboards and woodwind) have great-looking sites with lots of background information – but any sales enquiries are directed to local dealers. If you're looking to learn, online shops stock videotapes and books to help you. Sheet music libraries include tens of thousands of scores that you can buy or, for the ultimate net purchase, download and view or print direct from your computer.

ABC Music **www.abcmusic.co.uk**
Buy, sell or exchange your instrument at this Surrey-based shop.

Axemail **www.axe.music.co.uk**
Guitars, amps and drum machines – plus a new section for wind instruments.

Chappell of Bond Street **www.shopyell.co.uk/chappell**
Wonderful collection of sheet music covering all styles and instruments.

Churchill's Music **www.churchills-music.co.uk**
All the accessories you'll need for your synth or keyboard, but cumbersome ordering via email.

Don Mackrill's Music Stop **www.donmack.com**
Specialists in sax, brass and woodwind, but they also stock guitars and amps.

Drum Central Superstore **www.drumcentral.com**
Gongs to finger-cymbals and all the bass, hanging-toms and snares you can beat.

Hobgoblin Music **www.hobgoblin.com**
Bagpipes, flutes and citterns for people who like to sit in a pub playing Celtic reels, Irish jigs and the like.

Internet Music Shop **www.musicsales.co.uk**
Bright, friendly site filled with sheet music, tutoring systems and videos.

Saxophone Rental Company **www.saxophones.co.uk**
Hedge your bets by renting a sax instead of buying one when you learn.

Sheet Music Direct **www.sheetmusicdirect.com**
Stuck for something to play? Buy and download sheet music for instant inspiration.

//PETS

The British are famed as a nation of pet lovers. Other countries might eat the little furry or feathered things, but in the UK we traditionally admire, look after them – and even wrap them up in quilted jackets on cold winter nights. If you love pets, you'll find the Internet has a fantastic range of shops and informational sites that can provide all the accessories, bowls, leads, flea collars – and clothes – that your furry or feathered friend could wish for. And for fishy or reptilian pets, you can upgrade to a bigger aquarium, fit a new air pump or add a little sunken treasure. Many of the sites are aimed at children and include plenty of advice on caring for the pet.

Acme Pet **www.acmepet.com**
Vast catalogue of all the online shops selling things for pets, organised by species – plus advice on caring for and understanding the furry/winged/crawling/swimming beastie.

Animail **www.animail.co.uk**
Jolly pet shop that's fantastically easy to navigate and stocks masses for cats, dogs, birds and other small animals.

Aquatics Warehouse **www.aquatics-warehouse.co.uk**
Over 800 goods for ponds and aquariums, at around 25% off high-street prices.

Battersea Dogs Home **www.dogshome.org**
Meet the mutts and moggies waiting hopefully for a nice new owner. Or buy pet treats and T-shirts in the gift shop.

Doggie Bagz **www.doggiebagz.com**
Astonishing range of things for dogs – from bed to bowl, grooming and shampoo. Wonderful design.

Doggie Diamonds **www.doggiediamonds.com**
One for the dog crazy. Clothes and home furnishings with pictures of your favourite breed of dog.

Horseweb **www.horseweb.co.uk**
No frills horsey site that covers horses and tack for sale.

Pets Pyjamas **www.pets-pyjamas.co.uk**
Show your cat or dog that you care. Food, beds, grooming, books, treats, collars and healthcare – from one of the best-designed sites around.

Puppies and Dog Breeders **www.puppies.co.uk**
Books, get advice, insurance, food and grooming tips for cute puppies. Useful search function will lead you to an approved breeder, or you can place a wanted ad.

RSPCA **www.rspca.org**
Thinking of getting a pet? Visit the RSPCA first for essential advice for first-time owners.

SitStay GoOut store **www.sitstay.com**
Romp and jump and hunt and fetch accessories, equipment and goodies for your dog.

//PROPERTY

The Internet has helped take out the hard work and slog of finding a new house or flat. There are sites specialising in small islands, French farmhouses, country houses and city flats. The biggest sites use local agents around the UK to keep their databases up to date with thousands of houses and flats to buy or rent. And theres plenty of advice and checklists to help make your next move more manageable.

Unlike other shopping sites, you can't actually buy a property online (if one's offered, turn it down). You're using the net as a search tool, but you will still need to visit, view and have a professional survey on the property. And if you're looking for a mortgage for your future home, you can get pointers from the section in this book on money, but so far only a couple of lenders will let you sign up online for a mortgage – so again, you'll need to venture out into the real world to fix up a mortgage.

Asserta **www.asserta.co.uk**
Help buying your next home and an impressive database of homes for sale gathered from local agents.

Foxtons **www.foxtons.co.uk**
Upmarket agent provides plans, video clips and walk-throughs of its homes for sale.

Internet French Property **www.french-property.com**
Dream it, view it, buy it. An extensive selection of houses for sale and rent across the Channel.

Land.Net **www.land.net**

Lottery winners, step right up. Specialist sales of islands, castles and mansions. Exotic property and land that's available around the world.

Latitudes French Property **www.latitudes.co.uk**

C'est formidable! Over 3,000 homes for sale in France.

MSN HomeAdvisor **http://homeadvisor.msn.com**

One day, it'll all work this way. Stylish solution to finding a home and loan in the US.

PropertyFinder **www.propertyfinder.co.uk**

One of the most comprehensive databases online, compiling details from stacks of local and national agencies.

PropertyLive **www.propertylive.co.uk**

Run by the National Association of Estate Agents, this is a fast, searchable site for sales and lettings nationwide – plus plenty of advice to reduce the stress of moving.

Property Sight **www.property-sight.co.uk**

Best range of homes for sale in the UK. Local agents keep the 7,000 listings up to date, and you can register directly with them by email.

The London Office **www.thelondonoffice.co.uk**

Central listing of country properties. Or try Country Life (www.countrylife.co.uk)

Under One Roof **www.underoneroof.co.uk**

Clever display and virtual walkthrough of a dozen London properties for sale. Nice idea, but needs more houses and flats on its list.

Estate agents

Many traditional UK estate agents are online. Most now publish their property files online, but some use this to promote past triumphs rather than offer houses currently available.

Cluttons **www.cluttons.com**
Egerton **www.egertonproperty.co.uk**
Frank Knight **www.knightfrank.co.uk**
Friend & Falcke **www.friendandfalcke.co.uk**
General Accident **www.gaproperty.co.uk**
Hamptons **www.hamptons.co.uk**
John D Wood **www.johndwood.co.uk**
Strutt & Parker **www.struttandparker.co.uk**
Winkworth **www.winkworth.co.uk**

//SPORTS GOODS

Buy a bike, find a fishing rod or track down a tennis racket with the online sports superstores and specialist suppliers. And for dedicated sports fans, visit your top team's site to kit out with their latest strip. The sports chains tend to stick to selling sporty clothes and shoes, but specialist shops are the best place for range, if not discounts – although everyone beats the high-street prices.

Football teams

All the major football clubs have their own shops online. Find your team and stock up on the ever-changing kit, plus the usual key rings, biscuit tins and other bits and bobs:

Arsenal Shop **www.arsenal.co.uk**
Aston Villa FC **www.astonvilla-fc.co.uk**
Chelsea Megastore **www.chelseafc.co.uk**

Leeds United FC www.lufc.co.uk
Manchester City FC www.mcfc.co.uk
Manchester United Megastore http://shop.manutd.com
Newcastle United FC www.nufc.co.uk
Tottenham Hotspur FC www.spurs.co.uk
West Ham United FC www.whufc.co.uk
Wimbledon FC www.wfc.co.uk

Bikes

There are hundreds of bike shops online, thanks to the invention of mountain biking in the hills of California – right beside Silicon Valley. Tired webmasters can buy online then zoom up and down slopes. Here's a small selection of sites:

Aardvark Cycles **www.aardvarkcycles.com**
Vast selection of high-spec mountain bike equipment – from brakes to complete bikes. Customer-friendly site that ships around the world.

BikeAds **www.bikeads.com**
Virtual equivalent of the newsagent's window. Buy or sell your bikes and bits.

Bikesdirect.com **www.bikesdirect.com**
A reasonable range of low-price bikes, but the shopping is a bit fiddly.

CycleStore **www.cyclestore.co.uk**
Good range of bikes and accessories for cycling enthusiasts.

Sports

Action Fit **www.actionfit.com**
Design your own swimsuit or aerobic gear.

Adventure DooDads **www.adv-doodads.com**
You know how your rucksack fills up with those gadgets to hold ropes, carry water, pin things down and mend a broken arm? There're all for sale here.

Bass Pro Shops **www.basspro-shops.com**
Discount rods, tackle and ties to lure the fish – plus a mass of equipment for hunting folk and outdoor life.

Dragon Sports **www.dragonsports.co.uk**
Good range of cricketing clothes and kit.

Fishing Tackle **www.nimpopo.co.uk**
Discount fishing tackle – over 7,000 lines make this a great catch for any angler.

Happy Camper **www.ahappycamper.com**
Pack up your old kit bag from the fine range of items you'll need to live under canvas.

iGoFish.com **www.iGoFish.com**
Impressive range of flies and lures for fresh and saltwater fishing.

JD Sports **www.jdsports.co.uk**
Top site for sporting clothes and accessories from the high-street chain store.

Kitbag **www.kitbag.com**
Keeping up with your football team's latest kit is now easier, if no cheaper.

McLaren **www.mclaren.co.uk**
Support your favourite F1 team.

Newitts **www.newitts.com**
Badminton to football from the largest mail-order sports supplier in the country – nice pictures, good descriptions, but a rather sombre site.

ORP Rugby Shop **www.rugbyshopping.com**
Balls – but only a modest selection.

Petworth House **www.petworth-house.co.uk**
Indoor exercise machines, and some sports equipment.

RB Equestrian **www.rbe.co.uk**
Great selection of horse tack, feed and accessories.

Simply Scuba **www.simplyscuba.co.uk**
Not just snorkels and flippers, but everything for the serious diver, from cameras to wetsuits.

Soccerscene **www.soccerscene.com**
Best for footballs and boots, but they also do team strips and other bits of kit.

Tack and Ski **www.tackandski.co.uk**
Unusual combination of horse riding and skiing equipment and accessories. Just don't try to do both at once.

The Pro Shop **www.theproshop.com**
Clubs, bags and balls at discount prices, plus free delivery and the chance to try out that new niblick for 45 days before you decide to keep it.

Trout Fishing **www.ishop.co.uk/ishop/243/**
Stop by for gold heads, nymphs, streamers and the finest flies and lures.

Skinzwear **www.skinzwear.com**
Amazing (and fantastically skintight) swimsuits and active gear that only the confident can wear.

UK Golf Discount **www.ukgolfdiscount.com**
Everything for the golfer, cheap.

//TELEPHONES

Telephones are essential to the Internet. When you go online, you'll probably start with a standard phone line but developments by mobile phone networks will provide tight integration between mobile phones of the future and the Internet. You can already use the Internet to send short text messages to mobile phones (visit the network's site for details) and some phones now have web browsers and email software built in.

At the practical end for the consumer, mobile phones are now just another commodity item. You don't need a lot of advice, simply type in the amount of time you'll spend talking and compare prices from each network. Once you've chosen a network, the online shops can supply phones at low prices, normally saving money off high-street prices. If you want a mobile, there's a full choice plan from any of the major networks and the latest, tiniest phones to go with them. For trad phone users (called POTS – computer-speak for plain-old-telephone-system), you can pick up a new answering machine, phone or order a new telephone line. Almost all of the online electrical suppliers (see page 151) also sell standard phones, faxes and answering machines.

Major networks

Beyond 2000 UK **www.beyond-2000.co.uk**
Accessories for your mobile, together with satellite dishes and high-tech gadgets.

BT Shop **www.btshop.bt.com**
Connect with BT and shop from their range of phones, faxes and pagers. There's good advice on choosing the right equipment and a reasonable choice of models, but you'll find lower prices in specialist shops.

Cable & Wireless **www.cwcomm.co.uk**
All things telephonic, from one of the big players.

Carphone Warehouse **www.carphonewarehouse.com**
Mobile phones, pagers and accessories from the giant chain.

Cellnet **www.cellnet.co.uk**
Sign up and buy a phone online.

Direct Phones **www.direct-phones.co.uk**
Reasonable range of phones and accessories.

Miah Telecom **www.miah-telecom.co.uk**
Subscribe to any of the pre-pay or standard mobile tariffs from the major networks, with a good range of handsets.

Mobile Bargains **www.mobilebargains.com**
Good choice of pre-pay mobiles and top-up cards, accessories, car-kits and pagers.

One2One **www.one2one.co.uk**
Buy a new mobile online.

Orange **www.orange.co.uk**
Basic marketing and messaging services explained.

TalkingShop **www.talkingshop.co.uk**
Cheap mobile phones, with regular special offers.

Virgin Mobile **www.virgin.com/mobile**
Interesting phones and a good all-round package.

Vodafone **www.vodafone-retail.co.uk**
Subscribe and buy mobiles and accessories.

//TICKETS

Traditionally, you would order tickets for gigs, events or shows over the phone. Either direct with the venue or through a central booking agency. Now, the booking agencies (and a few of the venues) are online and provide the easiest, cheapest and sometimes the only way to pre-book tickets for any event.

Most of the online ticket agents combine a diary of events with the business of booking and paying for your ticket. Visit to find out when and where your favourite band is playing next, the dates for the football international or an opera performance. Once you've chosen your event, you'll see a list of types and prices of tickets available – normally relating to seating arrangements or place in the stadium. Choose the type of ticket you want and enter your credit card details. The ticket will be sent by post or, if you prefer, courier.

Aloud **www.aloud.com**

Tickets to any and every gig. Brilliant.

Concert Breaks **www.concertbreaks.com**

Tickets for concerts in the UK and Europe bundled with hotels and travel arrangements to make a package.

Lastminute **www.lastminute.com**

Don't plan ahead, and save a fortune. Great deals on top hotels, restaurants, concerts and flights.

Odeon **www.odeon.co.uk**

Pre-order tickets for the flicks. Use Scoot (www.scoot.co.uk) to see what the other cinemas are showing.

SceneOne **www.sceneone.co.uk**

Your local entertainment guide. Provides listings for TV, theatre, gigs and radio; find what you like, then buy the ticket (or the book or video).

theatre-link **www.theatre-link.com**

Ah, the roar of the greasepaint, the smell of the crowd ... what's on, how it's done and who performed. Good international coverage plus tickets and availability.

Ticketmaster **www.ticketmaster.co.uk**

Tickets for everything.

Tickets Online **www.tickets-online.co.uk**

Tickets to gigs, theatre and comedy shows.

Way Ahead Online Box Office **www.fortunecity.com/wayahead/**

Find out what's taking place, then buy a ticket. Covers gigs, comedy, theatre, classical music and sport.

What's on Stage **www.whatsonstage.com**

Instantly order tickets to any theatrical performance.

//TOYS

For time-pressed parents, there's plenty of choice from classic wooden train sets to the latest Barbie doll (did you know that each American girl has an average of eight?). Shop from around the world, so you can still buy the latest must-have even if they ran out of stock in the high-street months ago. The UK shops are a little disappointing on range – generally around 1,000 items seems the norm – but at least there's free delivery. The biggest, brashest and busiest sites are in the US – FAO Schwartz and Toysmart will give you a taste of what's available – and both will ship back to the UK. Choosing toys from your desktop means you won't have the fun of Saturday shopping with the children running riot, but at least you'll probably end up buying what you intended rather than what everyone else is screaming for.

A2Z Beanie Babies **www.a2zbeaniebabies.co.uk**

The entire range of these cutesie-wootsie little things.

Ace Toys **www.toy.co.uk**

Mad keen on toys? You'll love this site – a directory of specialist shops, a collector's corner, and toy news and gossip.

Acme Toys **www.acmetoys.com**
Vintage toys with a TV or cartoon pedigree – mostly high-quality collectibles out of reach of pocket-money budgets.

Action Man Island Command **www.actionman.com**
Kit out your action hero and play adventure games.

Alberon Dolls and Teddy Bears **www.dollycrafts.co.uk**
High-quality dolls and teddies that are probably too good for small, sticky paws.

Barbie.com **www.barbie.com**
One of the pinkest sites on the web. Buy a custom-made Barbie or design custom clothes for the one you have. There's even an exclusive Internet Barbie.

Bargain Beanies **www.bargainbeanies.com**
Cut-price Beanie Babies – with a good selection of quaintly named 'retireds' (that's second-hand).

Brain waves **www.brainwaves.co.uk**
Toys, videos and games to tease the brain into action.

Dawson & Son **www.dawson-and-son.com**
Step back to pre-plastic days with these wooden puzzles, blocks, toys, dolls' houses and jigsaws.

Disney **http://disney.go.com/shopping/**
All the merchandise and characters you'd expect from Disney.

FAO Schwarz **www.fao.com**
New York's wonderful toy store. Not quite the scale of rival etoy.com, but plenty of exclusives – and they ship around the world.

Funstore.co.uk **www.funstore.co.uk**
Confused parents can use a personal helper to find the perfect toy from the modest range put together by Hamleys.

Lego World **www.legoworld.com**
Build your own world with the full range from Lego Technic.

Letter Box **www.l-box.com**
Home of spinning tops, rocking horses and traditional toys.

Mail Order Express **www.mailorderexpress.co.uk**
Good range of toys on offer, and a nice feature that'll give you a list of gifts for a certain price. But there are no descriptions, photos or clues as to what half the stuff is.

Naturaltoys.com **www.naturaltoys.com**
For the traditional toy box, here's a huge range of natural (mostly wooden) toys that look good for the parents and are fun for the children.

Red Rocket **www.redrocket.com**
Jump on the Rocket for great toy ideas – backed up with a vast selection. They'll even wrap and ship the toy anywhere in the world.

Smart Kids Toys **www.smartkidstoys.com**
Creative, fun but challenging toys for children; great range, lots of help choosing the perfect toy – and free wrapping before it's shipped from Connecticut around the world.

Toy Chest **www.toychest.co.uk**
Toys for the pre-school set.

Toys Я Us **www.toysrus.co.uk**
Reasonable choice and low prices from the warehouse chain.

Toysmart.com **www.toysmart.net**
Vast range of over 10,000 educational toys for kids from birth and up – shipped from the US around the world.

Toy Town **www.toytown.co.uk**
Especially strong on outdoor toys for toddler to teenager with good descriptions and pictures to help confused parents decide.

TV Toys **www.tvtoys.com**

Find classic collectible toys from cult TV-shows of the seventies and eighties: stock up on models of the Banana Splits, The A-Team and The Avengers.

//TRAVEL

The travel agents on the high street are now under considerable pressure – on price and range – from their virtual rivals. You have access to the same booking technology as the agents and can save hundreds of pounds or dollars by doing it yourself. It takes just a few minutes to compare prices, check routes and times – then order and pay. Business travellers who want a complete service can store preferences of hotel chain, seating and food – then leave it to one of the clever website databases to arrange the best deal that also maximises your frequent flyer points. Wherever and however you're travelling, there are sites that will help you book and prepare for the journey.

For much more about holidays and travel, see the companion **Virgin Internet Travel Guide**.

Airlines

All the main airlines have their own sites. Many let you buy tickets online, but you'll probably find a cheaper price from one of the main online agents. If nothing else, you can check the flight times and join their frequent flyer schemes.

Aer Lingus **www.aerlingus.ie**
Aeroflot **www.aeroflot.org**
Air Canada **www.aircanada.ca**
Alitalia **www.italiatour.com**

American	**www.americanair.com**
British Airways	**www.british-airways.com**
British Midland	**www.iflybritishmidland.com**
Delta	**www.delta-air.com**
EasyJet	**www.easyjet.co.uk**
Go	**www.go-fly.com**
KLM	**www.klmuk.com**
Ryanair	**www.ryanair.com**
SAS	**www.sas.se**
TWA	**www.twa.com**
United	**www.ual.co.uk**
Virgin	**www.fly-virgin.com**

UK Train operators

Eurostar	**www.eurostar.com**
First Great Western Trains	**www.great-western-trains.co.uk**
First North Western	**www.firstnorthwestern.co.uk**
Great North Eastern Railway	**www.gner.co.uk**
Midland Main Line	**www.mml.rail.co.uk**
ScotRail	**www.scotrail.co.uk**
South West Trains	**www.swtrains.co.uk**
Thames Trains	**www.thamestrains.co.uk**
Virgin Trains	**www.virgintrains.co.uk**

Travel Agents

1Ski **www.1ski.com**

Where to ski and the best deals available for package deals. In the summer, try ice skiing in Europe.

A World of Holidays **www.worldof.net/holidays/**
Late deals, bargains and last-minute hols for the footloose and cash-strapped.

A2bTravel **www.a2btravel.com**
One of the best UK travel agent sites. Easy to search the guides, buy a plane ticket, book a last-minute holiday, sort out your ferry tickets or book a hotel.

Bags Etc Etc **www.excess-baggage.com**
Pack up your troubles in a new kit bag or trunk or holdall.

Bargain Holidays **www.bargainholidays.com**
Jaunty fun in the sun at cut-prices.

Biztravel.com **www.biztravel.com**
Maximise your frequent flyer points and make the most of your expense account trips. Great for business users, but not always the cheapest tickets.

Britannia **www.britannia.com**
Central directory of sites to help you plan, book and enjoy trips around the UK.

Cheap Flights **www.cheapflights.com**
Automatically scour over 30 agents to find the cheapest deal.

Christine Columbus **www.christinecolumbus.com**
Remember Christopher? Well, Christine packed his bags before he set off – here's her advice and products for women travellers.

ebookers **www.ebookers.com**
Don't wait in the phone queue, use this new website from travel agent Flightbookers for a great choice of cheap flights, cars, hotels and round-the-world tickets.

English Country Cottages **www.english-country-cottages.co.uk**
Rent a cottage for your hols – over 2,000 listed around England.

Epicurious Travel **http://travel.epicurious.com**
Upmarket site combines the style of Condé Nast's *Traveller* magazine with food, dining and online booking.

Eurostar **www.eurostar.com**
Travel to France and Belgium made very easy.

French Connections **www.frenchconnections.co.uk**
Over 400 rather nice homes to rent for your next holiday in France.

FrequentFlier **http://frequentflier.com**
Keep up to date with frequent flyer schemes.

Holiday Rentals **www.holiday-rentals.co.uk**
Holiday homes to rent around the world.

HotelWorld **www.hotelworld.com**
Find a hotel before you arrive, then book it online. Thousands of hotels in hundreds of countries.

Infotel **www.infotel.co.uk**
Where to stay in the UK – includes, unusually, guesthouses, with prices, location and rating. Online booking is antique but adequate.

There's a lot more travel advice and hundreds more essential websites in **The Virgin Internet Travel Guide**.

International Home Exchange **www.homexchange.com**
Swap your suburban semi for a palace.

International Student Travel Confederation **www.istc.org**
For students only – sign up for a card from your local ISTC office, then travel the world on cut-price tickets, staying everywhere cheaply and with easy work permits.

Kuoni Travel **www.kuoni.co.uk**
Smart long-haul hols around the world.

Lastminute.com **www.lastminute.com**
Don't plan ahead, and save a fortune. Great deals on top hotels, packages and flights.

Le Travel Store **www.letravelstore.com**
Arrive wrinkle-free with these own-brand clothes. Also worth trying is Travelsmith (**www.travelsmith.com**) for similar types of clothes.

National Express **www.nationalexpress.co.uk**
Book a bus trip throughout the UK-online timetables and bargain getaways.

Maps Worldwide **www.mapsworldwide.co.uk**
Find your way around any city or country.

TheTrainLine **www.thetrainline.co.uk**
Book your train ticket for any mainline journey with any operator within the UK.

Leisure Planet **www.leisureplanet.com**
See the hotel before you book; a vast collection of over 50,000 hotels, each with a mini slide show plus area guides.

MSN Expedia **www.expedia.msn.co.uk**
Everything you need to research destinations, book flights, hotels and cars instantly. Good design with piles of information from the Microsoft Network.

Places to Stay.com **www.placestostay.com**
Rates (in dollars) and reservations for hotels and B&Bs around the world.

Powells Cottage Holidays **www.powells.co.uk**
Tranquil cottage getaways in England and Wales.

Railtrack **www.railtrack.co.uk**
Clean, simple, efficient and it usually works. This site lets you search the timetables to plan your route by train, then links you to the local operator to book your ticket.

The Great British Bed and Breakfast **www.kgp-publishing.co.uk**
Switch from hotels to homes and save – a guide to the hundreds of B&Bs around the UK. Unfortunately, there are no ratings.

Thomas Cook **www.thomascook.co.uk**
Holidays, flights, currency and last-minute bargains from the high-street agent.

Travel Select **www.checkin.co.uk**
A simple, efficient travel agent.

Travelocity **www.travelocity.co.uk**
Just about the biggest travel agent on the web and powered by the same system that's used by the travel agents

WebFlyer **www.webflyer.com**
Choose your frequent flyer scheme with care, advises Randy. He'll tell you why and plenty more besides.

//OFFBEAT MUST-HAVES

There are plenty of weird things on the web, but – thankfully – surprisingly few are for sale. However, we've scoured the very edges of respectability to find some really very odd products.

Billy Bob Teeth **www.billybobteeth.com**
Choose hideous, wild buck false teeth and customise with stain levels. Similarly unpleasant dental extras can be purchased from www.rottenmouth.com.

Demotivators Calendar **www.despair.com**
Calendars of hopeless dates, demotivators for underachievers and other goodies for the terminally miserable.

Elite Titles **www.elitetitles.co.uk**
Step up in the world – buy yourself a title. Anyone can be a Lord, Viscount or Sir – not ancient titles, but using the old trick of changing your name by deed poll.

Enid Blyton **www.blyton.co.uk**
T-shirts and souvenirs for friends of Noddy and Big Ears.

EvolveFISH **www.evolvefish.com**
Gifts and toys for freethinking, anti-religious nuts you may know: the fire-belching nun and forthright signs provide a simple message of your beliefs to the preachers in society.

Gag Works **www.gagworks.com**
Free your inner child with a bulk order of stink bombs, itching powder and classic plastic turds.

Lunar Embassy **www.moonshop.com**
Buy a piece of the Moon for under $16.

Mind Gear **www.mind-gear.com**
The promise of accelerated learning, hypnosis and psychic trances from this range of sound brain-wave tapes.

Robot Store **www.robot-store.com**
All the stuff you'll need to build your own robot.

Spy Stuff **www.spystuff.com**
Paranoid or prying? There are bugs, stun guns, night vision glasses and even bomb detection kits here.

Star Registry **www.starregistry.co.uk**
Name a star after a loved one, just £55.

The Sorcerer's Shop **www.sorcerers-shop.com**
True love, riches, happiness and a perfect career with the help of these potions – direct from California.

Two Guys Fossils **www.twoguysfossils.com**
Real dinosaur fossils and replicas – whole beasties, skulls and other delights.

8//DUTY AND TAXES

When you shop, most of the goods you buy will attract extra duty or taxes payable to the government (although some goods, notably books and food, are free of tax). If you make a purchase from an online shop that's located outside your country of residence, your government will still expect to be paid taxes on what you've just purchased. However, since there are three different possible kinds of extra taxes to pay, it's fair to say that calculating the duty and taxes on something you have just bought is a nightmare.

The rates vary from item to item and from country to country. Most shoppers simply ignore the whole issue and get away without paying anything. However, it is a legal requirement to pay what's due – and in the UK the department responsible (Customs and Excise) has more power than any other governmental department, so you could wind up in court.

Here's our guide to the taxes and duty you should pay when you buy something on the Internet.

Ordering within the UK

If you buy something from a British shop and you are a UK resident, you'll only be liable for one tax: VAT. This is added to almost everything at a flat rate of 17.5%. Some goods, including books and food, are VAT exempt.

Ordering within the EU

Let's start with the relatively easy subject of the European Union (EU) – supposedly the free and open market. The EU consists of Austria, Belgium, Denmark, Finland, France (including Monaco), Germany, Greece, Irish Republic, Italy, Luxembourg, Netherlands, Portugal, Spain, Sweden and the United Kingdom.

If you buy goods from any of these countries and the item is posted to you in any EU country, you will only have to pay VAT (at your country's rate) on the imports. Unless, that is, you're buying alcohol, tobacco or perfume products – in which case you will also have to pay excise duty.

Electronic consumption

If you buy something for instant consumption that is not physically shipped to you, but instead is downloaded directly to your computer, the Customs and Excise calls this a 'service'. This applies to sound files (MP3), instant software purchases and videos. As a service, these purchases should only have VAT added to the bill.

Ordering from outside the EU

If you want to buy something from any other country, you will have to pay two, possibly three, sets of duties, as listed here:

- Customs duty – payable on goods brought into the country and charged at a variable rate.
- VAT – payable on most goods and usually charged at 17.5%.
- Excise duty – extra tax payable on certain goods, notably alcohol, tobacco and perfume.

The only exception is if you order an item that costs less than £18 (including postage). In this case, you don't have to pay customs duty or VAT (unless it's alcohol, tobacco or perfume, in which case you will still have to pay VAT and excise duty).

Who and when to pay?

Any parcel coming into the UK should have a customs label on it stating the value – the company sending out the parcel sticks this on. If there's no sticker or it looks fake, the customs department might open it to check.

The Post Office is responsible for calculating and collecting the charges for the duty and VAT due. They might also add on their own charges to cover time and handling on behalf of the customs department. You'll be charged these extras before you can collect the goods. If you had the item sent by courier (such as FedEx or DHL), you are likely to be told how much to pay by the courier company.

You might have noticed that we talk about 'should pay' and 'might pay'. The truth is that the Customs and Excise and the Post Office don't have the time to open every parcel that arrives in the UK. If it's a vast box with a big label stating its value, you'll probably get charged customs duty and VAT. The reality is that you are unlikely to be charged either.

You have a legal obligation to declare the amount you owe to the government (in practice, its collection agency – the Post Office). For most shoppers, it will be individual conscience rather than government policy that's the guide on whether to declare the amount owed.

VAT

VAT (Value Added Tax) is an extra duty that's payable on anything that's sold in or brought into the UK. Well, not quite everything – there are a couple of exceptions that are free of VAT: for instance, imported goods worth less than £18 (with the exception again of alcohol, tobacco and perfume). Everything else you buy will have VAT (the current rate is 17.5%) added to the total of the price plus any duty.

However, as we have noted, some goods are free of VAT, notably books and food. So, if you buy a book from Amazon.co.uk, you don't pay VAT but if you buy a CD from Boxman.co.uk, you'll see your receipt includes VAT as part of the total.

The USA has a similar tax, called State Tax. You'll see it on all the US shopping sites: if you are resident in the same state as the shop, you have to pay local State Tax (and if you're in New York, you get to pay two lots of tax to the two authorities). If you are based in the UK and order from a US shop, you don't have to pay local State taxes.

Excise duty

The second type of duty is charged on a specific group of products that includes alcohol, tobacco and perfumes. It is charged at different rates depending on the type of product (for example, alcoholic content). The supplier should be able to calculate this for you, but if not the customs department (or, more likely, your Post Office) will be happy to oblige!

Customs duty

If you buy something from a supplier based outside your own country, you will normally be liable to pay customs duty when bringing the goods back into your country (all countries will charge you customs duty when importing goods). This does not apply to goods bought within the EC or for goods where the total value is less than £18.

Personal allowance If you travel on holiday, you'll receive a personal allowance that lets you bring back a certain amount of alcohol, tobacco and so on without paying duty. This does not apply when shopping on the net; with only rare exceptions, whatever you buy will have duty liable and the amount you pay depends on the type of product. The rate varies up to a maximum of 17%.

//HOW MUCH DO I PAY?

Follow the steps below to work out how much you should be paying to import goods:

1 Check the duty rate and the VAT rate for the item you're planning to buy.

2 Convert the price you paid for the goods into UK sterling.

3 Multiply the sterling price you paid by the duty rate. This is the amount of duty you will have to pay.

4 Add together the duty and the original price you paid; multiply the result by the VAT rate. This result is the amount of VAT to be paid.

5 Finally, add together the duty and the VAT you've calculated – this is the total amount you should pay.

For example

Let's take a typical example – buying CDs. You're just about to buy a whole stack of CDs from the US. The total bill was £100. Here's what else you have to pay:

1 The duty rate is 3.5% and VAT is 17.5%.

2 You paid the equivalent of £100 sterling for your CDs.

3 The duty payable is £100 x 3.5% = £3.50.

4 We add the amount paid and the duty: £100 + £3.50 = £103.50. Multiply by the rate of VAT (17.5%), which comes to £18.11.

5 The total extra payable should be duty plus VAT: £3.50 + £18.11 = £21.61. You would normally pay this to the Post Office when collecting the goods.

Duty rates

There's a vast list of the rates you'll have to pay for different goods. Visit the UK Customs and Excise site for the complete list (**www.hmce.gov.uk**). The table on the next page illustrates just how variable the rates are – even within the same group of products. For example, if you like to ski, you'll pay more than a golf enthusiast. Similarly, if you're a musician, make sure you don't play an electric guitar. And as for clothes – only babies can afford to wear them!

//UK DUTY RATES PAYABLE ON IMPORTED GOODS

Commodity Group	Description	Full Rate Duty %	VAT %
Home Entertainment	CD players	9.5	17.5
	Records	3.5	17.5
	CDs	3.5	17.5
	Camcorders	4.9	17.5
	DVD players	14.0	17.5
	Video games	2.8	17.5
Computers	Including peripherals	0	17.5
Games & sport	Gymnastics/athletics/sports	2.7	17.5
	Golf clubs & balls	2.7	17.5
	Tennis rackets	2.7	17.5
	Skiing equipment	3.7	17.5
Clothes	Shirts	12	17.5
	Outergarments	13	17.5
	Undergarments	6.5	17.5
	Baby	10.5	0
Musical Instruments	String (other than piano & harp)	3.2	17.5
	Electric guitars	3.7	17.5
Skincare products	Including make-up	0	17.5
Spectacles	Including sunglasses	2.9	17.5
Toys	Construction sets: wood	4.5	17.5
	Construction sets: plastic	4.7	17.5
	Other	4	17.5

9//FAQS – FREQUENTLY ASKED QUESTIONS

As you start to use the Internet you're bound to come across questions, worries and problems and many of these are dealt with in the relevant chapters in the first part of this book.

In this section, we've covered the most commonly asked questions and their answers.

//THE CONNECTION

Q Why can't I connect?

A You've checked your modem's plugged in and switched on? Make sure that you have typed in the correct user name and password and are dialling the right telephone number.

Q Why does my modem keep dialling?

A Whenever you start a bit of Internet software (your web browser or email program), it automatically tries to connect to the Internet. If it can't connect, or the number's busy, it will redial a few times (normally five times).

Q Why do I keep getting disconnected from the net?

A It's likely that the idle timeout feature is cutting in. This will automatically disconnect you if the computer has not been used for a few minutes. Typically, this happens if you dash off to make a cup of tea or, more likely, you are reading a page without updating or browsing. Open the Control Panel and open the Internet/Connections icon; now change the 'Disconnect if idle for xx minutes' setting. It's also worth changing the same setting in the modem driver: in the Control Panel, open the Modems icon and click on the Properties button. The other problem is that your telephone line has the Call Waiting feature – this will upset your connection and might disconnect you (call your phone company to disable the feature). Lastly, make sure that someone else in the house isn't picking up a receiver to make an outgoing call when you're online – this, too, will disconnect you.

***Q* Why isn't my modem working at top speed?**

A First, make sure that you have the newest driver software for the modem. You might also find that there's a Flash upgrade for your modem. Visit your modem manufacturer's web site and download and install the driver or upgrade. For good advice on upgrades, try either **www.modem.com** or **www.modemhelp.com**.

***Q* I'm trying to dial out from the office but the modem reports there is no dial tone. Why?**

A Office phone systems (PBXs) don't normally supply a tone, confusing modems. You need to tell your modem to ignore dial tones and just dial by deselecting the 'Wait for Dialtone' option. Open the My Computer/Dial-up Networking folder and right-click on your connection icon to select Properties. Click on the Configure button, then the Connection page tag, and deselect this option.

***Q* When I connect to the Internet, the Dialer program tells me I've connected at 115Kbps – is this possible?**

A Your computer is transferring information to the modem at 115.2Kbps, the maximum speed possible with a standard computer, but the modem has connected to the Internet at the best speed it can negotiate. If the line's bad, the modem adjusts its speed down to ensure that the data doesn't get scrambled.

Q Is it likely that modems will run any faster than their current 56Kbps?

A Not really. That is, not really over a normal telephone line. In fact, it's actually illegal in the US to run a modem at 56Kbps (the max allowable is 53Kbps). Modems will gradually die off as cable modems, ADSL and other digital communications come into place.

Q Will my free ISP account last forever?

A It should do – but most free ISPs check that you've used your account on a regular basis. If you don't use the service for 90 days, they will probably cancel your account and you'll have to re-register.

Q How do I cancel my account?

A Check your contract with the ISP. Some will require a month's notice, others won't. Visit your ISP's main website and check the email address for the admin department. Send them an email telling them you want to cancel your account – and ask for an email to acknowledge this.

Q What's the best time to go online?

A Depends what's important to you. The cheapest time (in telephone costs) is evenings and weekends. The busiest time (and so the time when the web is slowest) is evenings and weekends. For top speed, connect when the US is asleep.

//INSTALLING SOFTWARE

Q My computer came pre-installed with Netscape and this automatically runs the AOL Instant Messaging system. I really don't want to chat to anyone, so how can I stop it running so that I don't get buzzed by friendly users when online?

A You can remove AIM totally from your hard disk, but keep it there for the moment – you might get a change of heart. However, if AIM runs automatically every time you connect to the Internet, it can be very annoying. Open the AIM window (click on the icon or choose Ctrl-9) then select the Setup/Misc menu option. From here, deselect the 'Start AIM when Windows starts' option. That's it.

Q **I've signed up with a free ISP that provides me with its own bundle of software – email, browser and newsgroup reader. Trouble is, I'm picky and want to try out other browsers and email programs. Will this work?**

A Yes. You can use any standard Internet software with a free account from an ISP that provides Internet access. For example, if you have a Freeserve account, you'll get Internet Explorer installed automatically. If you want to change to Netscape, just install Netscape. When you double-click on the Netscape icon it will automatically connect you to Freeserve. It's worth keeping the original software in place, in case of a problem, but you can delete it selectively using the Start/Settings/Control Panel option then double-clicking on the Add/Remove Programs icon.

//BROWSING

Q **Why does my web browser keep crashing?**

A It shouldn't. This probably means that you're not using the latest version of the browser. As new ways of enhancing web pages are developed, older browsers can find it hard to manage and simply stop working. Visit **www.microsoft.com** or **www.netscape.com** to download the latest version of your browser.

Q **Why isn't a web page there any more?**

A The website might have been closed down or, more likely, the designer has redesigned the site and reorganised the way the pages are stored and given them new names. If a page doesn't work, visit the main site's home page.

_Q_ What does 'Error 404 not found' mean?

A It means that the address of a web page does not exist. Either you typed in the wrong address or the site has been redesigned and the names of the web pages have been changed.

_Q_ Do all web page addresses start with the letters 'www'?

A No. You'll often see addresses that look very odd but will still work fine. The way addresses are created is slowly changing, so you can expect to see more addresses that are just names.

_Q_ I find the typeface far too small on many of my favourite web pages. Any solutions?

A You can increase the default, standard size of fonts used by your Netscape browser by pressing Ctrl-] to increase the size (and Ctrl-[to decrease the size). In IE use the View/Text Size menu option.

_Q_ What's a secure connection? How can I get one?

A Secure connections are set up by the web server (not by your web browser) – you can tell you've got a secure connection when the tiny closed padlock icon is displayed at the bottom of the screen.

_Q_ I saved some images from a website to my hard disk, now how can I view these GIF and JPEG format files on my PC?

A The simplest method is to use your web browser as the viewer. Start your browser (choose not to connect and to work offline) then start Windows Explorer. Click and drag one of the images from Explorer on to the browser and you'll see it displayed. The alternative is to use a paint program that's better than Paint installed with Windows – like Paintshop Pro **www.jasc.com**.

Q **What's a plug-in?**

A A plug-in is a special bit of software that adds a new feature to your web browser. For example, if you want to view video or animation in your browser, it needs to have a plug-in that supports this. If you visit a site that uses snazzy multimedia tricks and you don't have the right plug-in, you'll be told and given the chance to download the file required.

Q **I want to use bitmap images I created on my PC on my own web page. How can I do this?**

A You can, generally, only use GIF and JPEG format graphics files on a web page. You'll need to use an image editor program to convert your BMP format files to either GIF or JPEG. Try Paintshop Pro (**www.jasc.com**) or search **www.filepile.com**.

Q **I've been told to clean out my cache – why?**

A Your cache (pronounced 'cash') is a folder where your web browser temporarily stores the images and text files for the web page it's visiting. Most web browsers set aside tens of megabytes of hard disk space for the cache so that they can store thousands of web pages. The advantage is that next time you visit the page, the browser will pull up the files from your hard disk rather than from the slow web link. If your browser seems to run very slowly, your cache might be too big or too full. Choose the Options/Network Preferences menu in Netscape or View/Options/Advanced for IE users. You can now adjust the size of your cache (don't make it any bigger than 15–20Mb) or clear it.

***Q* I have downloaded a file that ends in the ZIP extension. When I double-click to run it, nothing happens. How do I open it?**

A A ZIP file contains a compressed version of the original file(s) that have been squeezed down to save space and time when downloading. To unzip your file, you'll need an unzip program. The best known is WinZip from **www.winzip.com**.

***Q* When I try to save a page with the File/Save As option in my browser, it just saves the text and layout – not the graphics. How do I capture the lot?**

A You need to use an offline browser that will grab all the associated files and store them on your hard disk. Try WebWhacker (**www.webwhacker.com**).

***Q* I have visited a few sites that play music samples and I would like to save these to my hard disk to play back later. How do I do this?**

A Most music is stored in the WAV, MIDI, MP3 or RealAudio file formats. To download and save any of these files, right-click on the link that plays the file and select Save Link As.

***Q* Should I be worried about cookies?**

A No, they are normally perfectly harmless. Most big sites use a cookie (it's a little file on your hard disk that lets a website store information on your machine) to store your name or preferences or the last time that you visited the site.

***Q* When I visit some sites, my browser tells me I need to download a plug-in. Should I?**

A These sites probably use animation, sound or video clips in their web design. If your browser cannot support these effects, it tells you and tries to download the appropriate plug-in (a little program that upgrades your browser). If you don't download the plug-in, the website will still work fine, but you'll not see the snazzy multimedia effects.

Q **I download lots of files from the Internet. I always check these with my virus scanner before I run the program, but what do I do with a compressed ZIP file?**

A When you unzip the contents of a ZIP file, it won't start any virus that's present; this means you can safely unzip the files and then run your normal virus scanner on the resulting files. However, if you're nervous about doing even this, you can ask the splendid WinZip utility (**www.winzip.com**) to scan the contents of a ZIP file before you open it up. Choose the Options/Program Locations menu in WinZip and enter the name of your virus scanning software. Now you can scan ZIP files from the Actions menu.

Q **How can I be sure to download a file as quickly as possible?**

A If you are downloading a file from a commercial site, such as CNET, you'll be given a list of various sites that store this file. You could choose the nearest geographic site, but use lateral thinking and pick a site in the world where it's still night-time – the traffic will be much lighter and your download should fly.

Q **Can I catch a virus by looking at a web page?**

A Viewing images, entering information in a form or just viewing text on a web page is perfectly harmless. That means 99% of all websites are fine. Sometimes you'll visit a website that uses snazzy multimedia or other trickery. You may be warned that your web browser needs to download a plug-in or Java or ActiveX applet (the name for a little program). These applets are normally developed to provide extra functions – such as shopping carts, multimedia or special effects. However, it is possible to write nasty little applets that trash the files on your computer. To avoid this, don't accept plug-in downloads from sites where you don't know the company.

Q Can I stop my kids viewing porn online?

A Yes, almost totally. Use one of the parental control programs such as NetNanny (www.netnanny.com) or CyberSitter (www.cybersitter.com) or, if you're on AOL, click on their Parental Control page. However, the best advice is to move the computer to the sitting room, where everyone can see it, and make sure you're in the room when they browse. They'll be too embarrassed to try.

//SHOPPING

Q Aren't I playing into the hands of thieves by paying with a credit card at an online store?

A No. Even Visa and MasterCard both say it's perfectly safe – so long as you shop sensibly. In fact, it's easier for a thief to pinch your card details when you pay at a restaurant or in a shop or by phone!

Q I've found a site that stocks something I want to buy – how do I know it's safe to proceed?

A The top rules for buying online are: (1) Only type in your credit card details if you're on a secure server (little closed padlock in the bottom corner of your browser). (2) Do you know the company name? If not, check further to find out the registered address and contact number – no contact phone number, no sale! (3) Check the policies on returns and guarantees.

Q Can I buy from any online shop?

A No. Many shops will only sell to people who live in that country.

This means that only US residents can buy from the majority of the US-based shops. All the shops listed in the main directory will ship around the world.

Q Is there anything that I cannot buy online?

A In theory, no – there's a shop for everything, however weird! In practice, you are more likely to hit incompatibilities or customs problems. For example, US videotapes won't work in the UK and, if you want to order a banana tree from California, customs in the UK won't allow it into the country for fear of spreading disease.

Q Are warranties and guarantees the same for items bought on the net?

A Yes, unless it's otherwise specified. The only exception is to (normally electronic) products you've bought from outside your country. For example, if you live in the UK and buy a computer in the US, it's very unlikely the warranty will be honoured.

Q I'm trying to find the best range of shops that sell cigar cutters – what's the best strategy?

A Forget about using one search engine at a time. Instead, use Google (**www.google.com**) to automatically search a dozen of the top engines at the same time. It'll return a neat list of sites that cover cigar cutters, as indexed by AltaVista, Excite! InfoSeek, Lycos and Yahoo!

Q How do I find the cheapest prices?

A The US is the land of the bargain-finding website. The best site is MySimon (**www.mysimon.com**). It will scan dozens of online shops for a particular product and then list the cheapest suppliers. In the UK, there's ShopSmart (**www.shopsmart.com**)

and MyTaxi (**www.mytaxi.co.uk**) – but these are limited to searching for the cheapest books, videos and CDs.

***Q* How do I find other, similar shops that stock the same sort of goods.**

A Wade through the results of a search engine or, better still, leave it to Alexa (**www.alexa.com**). Once installed – and it's now part of Netscape Communicator – Alexa sits in your browser's toolbar and lists other sites that are similar to the one you're visiting. Alternatively, if you're using Microsoft's IE v5 browser, choose the Tools/Show Related Links.

//EMAIL

***Q* Why does an email get returned as 'undeliverable'?**

A You've typed in the wrong email address when you created the message. Check with your friend that you have their correct address – it should be in two parts: their name or nickname, an '@' symbol and their company or ISP name. For example, 'response@virgin-pub.co.uk'. Some addresses have full stops or underscore '_' symbols – type this in as well.

***Q* What can I do about junk mail?**

A Unsolicited junk mail – called spam – is the bane of life with email. Dumb companies send out millions of messages in the vain hope of marketing themselves. Many ISPs now have anti-spam systems in place that automatically recognise known culprits and reject any mail received from them. You don't have to do anything – but check with your ISP to see if they have this feature. Alternatively, if you keep getting junk mail from a particular address, you can create a new filter (or rule) in your email program that automatically deletes any message from this person as soon as it's received.

***Q* I've joined a mailing list but now I want to get off. Unfortunately, I've deleted the original instructions that tell me how to unsubscribe from the list. What can I do?**

A Visit the **www.liszt.com** site and search for your list. Under the description, it should give you instructions about how to subscribe and unsubscribe to the list. If not, see if there is an admin email contact and send them an email.

***Q* Can anyone else read the emails I send?**

A Email messages are sent in plain text form – as you typed it out. As the email passes across the Internet, malicious system managers could, in theory, read it. However, with hundreds of millions of mail messages zipping around the net every day, it's unlikely. If you want to make quite sure that the head of IT in the company isn't peeking at private post, scramble the contents of your messages. The most secure system around is called PGP (**www.pgp.com**), although most email programs have some form of encryption built in.

***Q* What do I do if someone's harassing me by email?**

A Tread carefully. If it's an unknown nut, it might be better not to reply (this can wind them up even more); change your email address – get a free account – and tell your ISP that you've been getting this type of email. They are in a better position to try and track down the sender and automatically block any further email.

***Q* I have been offered a mailing list with millions of email addresses on it. Should I send them all news of my new wonder product?**

A No. It's called spamming and it's horrible. It's also killing the net by slowing everything down. Lastly, you'll be thrown off your ISP and your company name will be mud. That should be pretty clear!

//NEWSGROUPS AND CHAT

Q Where can I find the newsgroups that my ISP doesn't handle?

A Visit Deja (**www.deja.com**) to read what's been said in all the newsgroups, or visit Jammed (**www.jammed.com**) for a list of news servers that will let anyone access all the newsgroups.

Q Will I get junk mail if I post a message to a newsgroup?

A Some unscrupulous companies comb the newsgroups to pick up the email addresses of users, then sell these on as mailing lists, so you may well get junk mail. If your ISP provides you with more than one email address (most do), reserve one for your newsgroup activity and ditch any unwanted mail received on that address.

Q I posted a message a few days ago, now it's gone. What's happened?

A So many messages are posted every day that your ISP's computer has to delete messages after a few days to save space.

Q How can I search for old newsgroup messages?

A You need to use one of the archive sites, such as Deja (**www.deja.com**), which stores copies of messages from all newsgroups.

Q Can I write a test message before diving in?

A Yes, use the alt.test newsgroup – don't write test messages to a normal newsgroup or you'll get a lot of rude replies.

Q I want to try IRC (Internet relay chat) but how do I find a server that lets me use this?

A Ask your ISP – they should have an IRC server. Alternatively, when you install your IRC software, it will have a list of IRC servers that you can use or you can search Liszt (**www.liszt.com**) for a server near you.

Q How do I find out when a celeb will be online and available to chat?

A The best place to look is Yack (**www.yack.com**). It lists the times and places for scheduled celebrity chat sessions.

Q How can I have a private chat with friends?

A IRC is a very public place to chat, so you'll need to use one of the instant messaging systems – a popular system is ICQ (**www.icq.com**), which gives you plenty of privacy.

//GLOSSARY

access provider See ISP.

address book A list of names and their email addresses. Your email program provides this feature to let you manage your contacts.

alias An alternative name you use in either chat or email (or both).

applet A small program that's downloaded from a website and runs within your web browser. Some online shops implement their shopping cart system using an applet.

attachment A file sent with an email message.

authentication Method of identifying a company as being who or what it claims to be. This is usually done through a system of certificates (issued by independent companies such as VeriSign – **www.verisign.com** – and Thwate – **www.thwate.com**)

authoring Creating a web page.

bit A basic storage unit used in computers; a bit can only be one of two values '1' or '0'. Data is stored in a computer as a combination of bits (eight together are referred to as a byte). Bits are normally used when specifying the transmission speed of a modem (for example, 56Kbps means 56,000 bits sent every second).

body The main text part of an email message.

bookmark A way of storing the address of an interesting website in your web browser. When you want to revisit the site, don't bother typing in the address, just click on the bookmark entry. Microsoft calls this feature 'Favorites'.

bps Bits per second. See 'bit'.

browser Special software that you need to view a web page and navigate through the web. The two main browsers are Netscape Navigator and Microsoft Internet Explorer.

byte A basic unit for storing data in a computer; a byte is made up of eight separate bits and can store numbers between 0 and 255. Your computer's memory and hard disk storage capacity is normally measured in bytes – in a document, one byte would be used to store one character. Compare this with 'bit'.

certificate A way of proving that the website you are visiting is owned by the company declaring ownership. This process is referred to as authentication (see) and is used in secure web servers. The certificate is actually a unique set of numbers that has been granted by a trusted company (such as VeriSign or Thwate) – but only once they are satisfied that the company is legitimate and authentic.

CGI (Common Gateway Interface) An advanced feature of website programming that allows a web page to send information to a program running on the server. For example, if a web page has a search feature, the search term you enter on the web page is sent to the search program using CGI.

cookie A tiny scrap of information stored on your computer by a website. Sounds very much like big-brother stuff but it's actually used by shops to store information such as when you last visited the shop, your last order number or account number. Normally totally harmless and sometimes necessary for a shopping site to work at all.

Dial-up A connection to the Internet that is not permanent: you need to dial a number to make the connection (just like using a normal phone). If you get an account with an ISP, it's usually a dial-up account – this means you can get online using a modem.

digital certificate See 'certificate'.

domain name The unique name that identifies one website or computer on the Internet. For example, the domain name 'microsoft.com' identifies the server provided by Microsoft.

domain name system (DNS) A method of converting the domain name to the IP address (a series of numbers) that's actually used to locate the computer. The list of names and addresses are stored on a domain name server (also called DNS). For example, if you type in the domain name 'www.microsoft.com' in your web browser, this is passed to a DNS that translates the name to a set of numbers that points to the Microsoft server.

email (electronic mail) Way of sending text messages, files and video clips to another user on the Internet. But you'll need to know their unique email address.

e-wallet Feature of new web browsers that lets you enter a range of different ways of paying for your shopping. You might include your credit card and e-cash, then open your e-wallet when you visit a shop. It's one future method of managing your spending on the net.

FAQ Frequently Asked Question.

folder In an email program, this refers to a container for your email messages or, on a hard disk, it's a container for files.

FTP (File Transfer Protocol) Protocol used to transfer files between computers over the Internet.

Gateway A link between two different systems. For example, an email gateway can be used to resend an email message to a fax machine or pager.

GIF A common graphics file format used to store images on a web page.

gopher An older system that allowed users to navigate the Internet – it's now almost entirely replaced by the web and you're very unlikely to see it in action – unless you get caught up on an academic server.

Hayes AT The set of commands used to control almost all modems. You shouldn't need to deal with the AT command set, but if you do: 'ATDT 123' means dial '123', 'ATH' means hang up. Visit modem manufacturer Hayes' site (**www.hayes.com**) for more information.

header The part of an email message that contains the recipient's address, sender's name, subject of the message and any delivery options.

home page The first page you see when you visit a website, before proceeding to other documents and links. The home page is normally stored in a file called 'index.html'. If you visit **www.microsoft.com**, you are actually viewing the Microsoft home page on its website.

HTML (Hypertext Markup Language) The set of codes that are used to layout and format a web page. These codes let you add links, define text styles, use colours and insert images into a page.

HTTP (Hypertext Transfer Protocol) The series of commands (protocol) used by a web browser to ask an Internet server for a particular web page. You'll see this at the start of most web addresses (though you don't have to type it in) to identify this **address** as a web page rather than a file (which uses a sister protocol, FTP).

hyperlink/hypertext A way of linking web pages together across the web. One word or image in a page can be linked to any other page on the site or any other site on the web. When the user clicks on the link, they jump immediately to the referenced page. It's the way you browse and surf the web.

Internet (or net) The millions of computers that are linked together around the world so that each can communicate. The Internet is public, so any user can visit any other computer linked to the Internet.

Internet service provider see ISP.

intranet A mini, private Internet within a company. Employees can browse their company information in just the same way as you would on an Internet using a web browser.

IP (Internet Protocol) The key to the way computers on the Internet can locate each other and communicate. An IP address is a string of numbers that identifies each of the main server computers on the Internet. To make it easier for users to manage an IP address, it's translated into a friendlier text form, called a domain name.

ISDN A high-speed digital version of your standard old phone line. You'll get a speedy connection to the Internet using an ISDN link, but you need a special modem (called a Terminal Adapter) and an

ISP that provides ISDN access for its users. ISDN, however, is being overtaken by the new cable modem and ADSL technology.

ISP (Internet Service Provider) A company that provides a doorway on to the Internet for you, the user. When you subscribe, you'll get a set of telephone access numbers (called PoPs) that your modem can dial to link to the Internet. Most ISP companies provide access numbers in one area or country; a few provide global access numbers. If the ISP also publishes its own mass of information for its users, it's called a content provider – the biggest of these content providers are AOL and CompuServe.

JPEG A file format used to store the graphic images displayed on a web page; JPEG files are usually used for photographic images, GIF files are better for simple images with fewer colours.

Kbps Kilobits per second, i.e. 1,000 bits of information sent every second – used to measure the speed of a modem or other communication devices. See also 'bit'.

mail server A computer on the Internet that deals with your email: storing your incoming mail until you login and read it and passing on the email messages you send to the right address. Your ISP will provide you with the address of its mail server. You'll need to configure your email software to look at this address for your new mail.

MIME (Multipurpose Internet Multimedia Extensions) A way of sending a file within an email message. In the old days, you would have to encode any file attachment before sending it over the net. Now, MIME is the standard used to painlessly and automatically send files between users.

Modem A special device that connects your computer to a telephone line and allows you to dial and connect to an ISP – and so gain access to the Internet. A modem works by converting your computer's data into sound signals that can be sent along a phone line. New communication systems (like ISDN, ADSL and cable modems) do away with this conversion and send information in its native digital format to provide much higher transfer speeds.

name server A special computer on the Internet that converts a domain name to its IP address. See 'DNS'.

Netscape Navigator One of the most popular web browsers on the market – get a free copy from **www.netscape.com**.

newsgroup A public discussion forum that lets anyone discuss a particular subject, hobby or interest. There are over 60,000 newsgroups that, collectively, are called the Usenet. They provide one of the most active areas of the Internet – you'll need a newsgroup reader (which should be built into your web browser) to read and submit messages.

PGP (Pretty Good Privacy) A way of encrypting an email (or file) so that only the intended recipient can decrypt it and read the message – used by some small shopping sites to enable customers to safely send in their credit card details.

PoP (Point Of Presence) A telephone number (provided by your ISP) that your modem dials to connect to their computer and so to the Internet. Make sure that your ISP provides PoPs in your local area and that these are local numbers.

POP3 A method of transferring email messages over the Internet. The POP3 standard is normally used to retrieve your messages and the SMTP standard is used to send the mail. IMAP is a new standard that's set to replace both POP3 and SMTP over the next few years.

post office See mail server.

protocol A set of rules that define the way something happens. For example, the POP3 system of sending mail is a protocol that defines the commands used to actually transfer the message.

secure site A shopping site that provides a system (almost always the SSL standard) to ensure that there is a secure channel between the site and your browser – anything you type in (such as your credit card details) cannot be unscrambled or read by a hacker.

SET (Secure Electronic Transmission) New rival to the established SSL standard that provides a secure way of sending your payment details over the net to a shop.

shopping cart/basket An electronic equivalent of the wire basket you use in your supermarket. Lets you add items as you browse a shopping site, then move to the checkout to pay.

SMTP Simple mail transfer protocol. See POP3.

SSL (Secure Sockets Layer) A way of scrambling the data between your web browser and the website so that no hacker and eavesdropper can read the information you are sending. Normally used on a web page that asks you to enter a credit card number or personal details. Your browser will indicate a secure, SSL page by displaying a tiny closed padlock icon in the bottom line of the windows. Don't shop without this!

TCP/IP (Transmission Control Protocol/Internet Protocol) The rules that describe how all information is sent over the Internet and how it finds its way to the right destination.

UART (Universal Asynchronous Receiver/Transmitter) A special chip in your computer responsible for sending and receiving data in a serial form – which means anything sent via a modem.

URL (Uniform Resource Locator) The correct name for the full address of a web page. For example, 'microsoft.com' is a domain name, 'www.microsoft.com' is the website address for Microsoft and 'www.microsoft.com/index.html' is the URL to the site's home page.

Usenet The collective name for the mass of over 60,000 newsgroups on the Internet.

UUencoding An older method of converting files into a special format before attaching them to an email message. Thankfully, this is now done automatically.

web browser A software program that lets you view a web page and navigate around the web.

web page A single, individual page within a website. Each web page is stored in a separate file; the file contains HTML commands that describe the text, its layout, formatting and links.

web server A computer that stores a website (generally, web servers store hundreds of separate websites or, in the case of mammoth sites from the BBC or CNN, the website is big enough to deserve its own web server.

website A collection of web pages produced by one person or company and about a particular subject.

//INDEX

//C

//D

//T

//V

//W

//Y

//OTHER GREAT VIRGIN INTERNET GUIDES

The Virgin Guide to the Internet
The advice you need to plug in, log on and get going.

The Virgin Family Internet Guide
Get the best out of the Internet – and lock out the worst.

The Virgin Internet Travel Guide
The complete guide to destinations and deals.

The Virgin Internet Music Guide
The web is alive – with the sound of music.

The Virgin Internet Money Guide
Get your finances sorted online.

The Virgin Internet Business Guide
The essential companion for anyone in business.

The Virgin Weird Internet Guide
It's a crazy world out there.

The Virgin Internet Auction Guide
Bid for an online bargain.

The Virgin Internet Research Guide
How to find out just about anything on the net.

The Virgin Internet Guide for Kids
Adults – keep out!

For more information, ask your local bookseller – or check out
http://www.virginbooks.com

www.rightmove.co.uk
assertahome.com
www.spie.co.uk
www.bradleys-estate-agents.co.uk
www.friendsreunited.co.uk
(CPKC).

www.creteproperty.co.uk

jjholland@hotmail.com

glenlear@yahoo.com
dunny@eurobell.co.uk
fish4.com